Praise for *BECOMING A MAN*

"Nearing its final pages, I had scrawled so many questions in the margins that I began to question the nature of my curiosity. A new thought emerged: that this is one of the risks and delights of a good memoir. If the writer has done the job well, the reader falls in love—and one principal feature of love is that it craves access to every part of you."

—*The New York Times Book Review*

"Elegiac and celebratory, this memoir charts how the author's gender transition upended both his marriage and his notions of masculinity: 'I am a work in progress, always doubling as different selves in different spaces, still learning how to navigate the multiple truths this body inhabits.'"

—Oprahmag.com

"This moving narrative illuminates the joy, courage, necessity, and risk-taking of [Carl's] gender transition and the ways his loved ones became affected and eventually enriched by it. A passionate, eloquent memoir about how 'complex stories of humanity [and] our capacity for imagination are what give us hope.'"

—*Kirkus Reviews*

"In this deeply personal and moving debut memoir, theater writer Carl shares the story of his difficult yet triumphant gender transition. . . . Carl's honest, timely musings illustrate the deep ruminations that can arise about one's assigned gender at birth and the gender one becomes. Carl's thoughts about sexuality and his compassionate feelings for sexual assault survivors will captivate readers from the first page to the last."

—*Publishers Weekly*

"An informative, fast, and fascinating read."

—*The Arts Fuse*

"A brave, raw account of the author's journey toward embracing his maleness."

—Washington Independent Review of Books

"A frank and heartfelt memoir about one man's transition offers insights into how people experience and understand gender."

—Shelf Awareness

"[Carl] writes with the directness and intimacy we yearn to encounter in conversation. *Becoming a Man* is a memoir that is jolting, honest, passionate, and beautifully written."

—Claudia Rankine

"Raw and honest, probing and skeptical, P. Carl's *Becoming a Man* is thoroughly compelling—a deeply moving meditation on love, loss, and what makes a self."

—Elizabeth Kolbert

"*Becoming a Man* is a fierce and thoughtful memoir of a transitioning body. In grappling with his own biology, gender theory, politics, and relationships, P. Carl has proven himself an indispensable voice in the conversation around gender identity. His story is a galvanizing call to action: to love, embrace, and fight for transgender lives."

—Joey Soloway, creator and showrunner of *Transparent*

"This book is both devastatingly honest and a joyful triumph. P. Carl communicates empathy on a cellular level. Everyone interested in gender, the body, and the resilience of the human spirit should read his book. It is rare for a book to equally address the gut, the mind, the heart, and the body with so much insight, honesty, and love. Not only a memoir of a transition, this book is a searing look at what it means to be a man in America in 2019."

—Sarah Ruhl, playwright of *The Clean House*

"In *Becoming a Man*, P. Carl movingly and incisively conveys experiences that range from self-perception to mortality itself, experiences that matter to all of us, regardless of our sexual identities. *Becoming a Man* is a profound human story."

—Michael Cunningham, author of *The Hours*

BECOMING A MAN

THE STORY OF A TRANSITION

P. CARL

SIMON & SCHUSTER PAPERBACKS

New York London Toronto Sydney New Delhi

Simon & Schuster Paperbacks
An Imprint of Simon & Schuster, Inc.
1230 Avenue of the Americas
New York, NY 10020

First Simon & Schuster paperback edition January 2021

SIMON & SCHUSTER and colophon are registered trademarks of Simon & Schuster, Inc.

For information about special discounts for bulk purchases, please contact Simon & Schuster Special Sales at 1-866-506-1949 or business@simonandschuster.com.

The Simon & Schuster Speakers Bureau can bring authors to your live event. For more information or to book an event, contact the Simon & Schuster Speakers Bureau at 1-866-248-3049 or visit our website at www.simonspeakers.com.

Interior design by Jaime Putorti

Manufactured in the United States of America

10 9 8 7 6 5 4 3 2 1

Library of Congress Cataloging-in-Publication Data has been applied for.

ISBN 978-1-9821-0509-9
ISBN 978-1-9821-0510-5 (pbk)
ISBN 978-1-9821-0511-2 (ebook)

For Lynette—resilience, strength, beauty

and LeAnn

and Lenny

CONTENTS

Becoming foreign. To yourself and others. So that's what a transition looks like.

—Jenny Erpenbeck, *Go, Went, Gone*

CHAPTER ONE

FINALLY ME

NEW YORK, NEW YORK

When bodies gather as they do to express their indignation and to enact their plural existence in public space, they are also making broader demands; they are demanding to be recognized, to be valued, they are exercising a right to appear, to exercise freedom, and they are demanding a livable life.

—Judith Butler, *Notes Toward a Performative Theory of Assembly*

I have been living as a white, Midwestern woman for fifty years and ten months, until one weekend in March, I cross a line. It comes unexpectedly on this particular day, but I've been thinking and expecting it for as long as I can remember. The Hotel Chandler in Midtown Manhattan: seven months on testosterone, I check in at about 6 P.M. "Good evening, sir, how are you?" This isn't my first "sir"—they have come and gone my entire life, and more often in recent weeks. But it's the start of something that from this "sir" forward will be my new life. On March 16, 2017, I become a man.

What changed from yesterday and the day before yesterday? What is this fine line of gender that makes me a woman one day and a man the next? Did my jawline get just square enough, my voice deep enough? Did my hairline recede enough? All I know is that from March 16 forward, I am finally me. I take a selfie and send it to my wife, with a text message: "I'm me now." I can't fucking believe it. I am finally me. I am visible for the first time, just two months shy of my fifty-first birthday. This rite of passage, this moment of being welcomed into the world as embodied is something most people experience at the moment of birth, or even earlier, at the moment of those ultrasound pictures of unborn babies that all my friends with children have, already sexed by their obstetrician and their parents. Some of us are never announced into the world and some of us wait fifty years.

I am finally announced into being in this moment in a random hotel in Manhattan unraveling my past, present, and possible future. There are so many political ramifications of this new body—ramifications I both know and can't know until I begin to live them.

The next morning, I will go down to the hotel restaurant for breakfast. "Good morning, sir, what can I get you? Coffee, sir?" I will read the news on my phone: a white supremacist is being asked to resign from the White House; it's the lead story. Second up, another judge has granted a temporary restraining order on the president's newly revised travel ban, from seven countries to six. This judge also thinks it is discriminatory, even with Iran dropped from the list. My waiter is from India I learn after he brings me my oatmeal; he tells me he and his wife recently immigrated here. Just in time, I think to myself. They both work at the restaurant. He forgets to bring me my orange juice. I will get free breakfast for the rest of the week, with many apologies to this newly minted white man. When I ask for more coffee, he calls me "boss," a term I will hear often from now on from men of color in service positions: valets, waiters, taxi drivers. I am stunned and embarrassed by the term, the sudden privilege and power that emanates from my white male skin. I don't feel it in my body yet. But the world can see it.

I come into being as a white man in 2017. White male supremacists occupy the White House. Immigrants are deported and denied entry to the United States. Black lives don't matter to the politicians controlling Congress. I am announced to the world as a man eight months before #MeToo will fill our social media and news feeds—women will unsilence themselves and begin the arduous process of dismantling the lives of individual men, one by one by one, for unspeakable acts of discrimination, harassment, assault, and abuse. No part of this two-year stretch has been more divisive than the Republican Party's insistence on appointing Brett Kavanaugh to the Supreme Court. No moment has been more despairing than listening to Susan Collins, a woman, a senator, say that Christine Blasey Ford was likely assaulted but that it wasn't by Kavanaugh—to hear one woman say to another woman that she doesn't believe her, among a chorus of white men who decry what has been done to Kavanaugh, that he is the victim, not Blasey Ford. Depending on who sees me and in what context, my body is grouped with these men and Collins in this moment in history—a threat not just to women but also to a fragile democracy on the brink of collapse, in part over a gender divide that has never been more volatile.

This book is a layperson's anthropological exploration of living a double life, Double consciousness, to borrow a term from W.E.B. Dubois, is a permanent condition of a trans person who has lived a life in one body and then another. The nuances of doubling require an untangling of two bodies, two distinct perspectives, two lives lived. I seek to do justice to the complexity of this emotional travel as I write this book in a number of different cities and through an evolving bodily transubstantiation where in one moment I am material subject matter to be consumed and in another I feel like a holy essence, my body and blood both sacrificed and blessed into being.

For most of my life, this process of becoming feels lethal, the disparate parts always at war with one another. I am born to the name Polly, but I never feel like her. I spend decades trying to know her, shape her into something that I can bear to live with. I medicate her, I dress her like I imagine Carl would look if he were allowed to live. On two occasions, I try to kill her off. The moment at the Hotel Chandler when I am lifting my hands over my head and jumping up and down and taking photos and posting them everywhere is the beginning of revelations, the ones I will try to convey to you in these pages. I become solid enough to share with you how my becoming is filled with contradictions and questions, and sometimes I have the courage to look back and tell you about what Polly went through and other times I want to convince you I was always only Carl.

I purposely choose a name to reflect my past and present. I don't know all the ways this name will matter to the life that will unfold when I choose it. I do know that I am fifty-one when I change my name. I can't imagine suddenly being summoned as Paul, or my favorite Italian name, Giacomo, Jack in English. I know that if I heard these names at this stage in my life, I wouldn't recognize them as me. Polly Kathleen Carl. What parts of her can I keep? My father and brothers have often mistakenly been called Carl, as if their last name might be their first. P. Carl is continuity. I hold on to a piece of her and acknowledge that he has always been with me. I had no idea the trouble this name would cause the world. It crashes the computer systems at the pharmacy and the airport. It makes my passport look like it's missing a first name and at every border crossing I must convince the customs agent that this is me. Each exchange requires a shift in vantage point for what can constitute a name. "Yes, this is really my legal name," I say over and over. "I go by Carl." Though the first time we meet, people insist on calling me "P," as if what is first in the order of a name must always come first.

This is also a book about changing a name, a life, and a gender—crossing a seemingly indistinguishable line and all the implications of that crossing—for me, my family, my friends—in an American political landscape that misunderstands transgender bodies even as some progress is being made toward accepting that we exist, we are human, and we deserve a livable life. I lived half a century first as a girl and then as a queer woman, and now for almost two years as a man. What does it mean for a body to transform? Do those changes transform an inner life, a person, and his personality? Am I fifty-two years old? Or have I just been born? What do you see? What do I feel? What do I know about America's fraught relationship with gender having inhabited these two bodies? Is there a revolution lurking in my double consciousness, in transgender bodies, that might reinvent discussions of gender? Can I, can other white trans men, bring something new to the conversation about white masculinity? In the words of Christine Blasey Ford, an American hero, my purpose in coming forward is to be "helpful."

If you had asked me five years ago, before I started taking testosterone, "Are you a man?" I would have said no. I would have said, as I wrote in an essay at the time, "A Boy in a Man's Theatre," that I was a boy—that I had missed the rites of passage to adulthood because I was never a girl and never a woman, and I didn't want the baggage that comes with being a man. I desired to live in perpetual boyhood because boys are infinitely more likable than men.

Everyone around me was comfortable with this. They liked the image of me as a boy. I looked the part—youthful, short-haired, and short in stature, dressed in little tailored suits. My wife joked, "You dress like a businessman, a tiny toy businessman." The last lines of my wedding vows to Lynette from 2012 were, "And I own these words now and say them with all the conviction a boy can muster: I love you, Mary Lynette D'Amico, and vow to do so forever and always." As long as I stayed in the container of my female body, I could call myself a boy and still be a heroic woman, happily married to Lynette, challenging men and their dominance in my profession and inside my family.

It's an important distinction, and one I didn't understand until I crossed over from boy to man. In the queer community, boy is an affectionate term; the slang boi is used as another way to refer to younger or perhaps "less butch" butches. Butches and bois aren't men, they are queer women. Lesbians, my wife for example, have expressly defined their desire in opposition to men but not to butches and to boys (that is, tomboys). When women marry butches and boys, they are still marrying women on the legal certificates.

Boys also have less accountability than men. I keep thinking of the family of the president. His two older sons are men and get called out for hunting endangered species, for lying, for being sexist. But the youngest son is only twelve. I don't know what he does, but there is a consensus that he's off-limits to a certain degree because he's a boy. There is an accountability that comes with white adult masculinity, and if you've spent your life minimizing your contact with it and its power over you, suddenly being confronted by a white man in a marriage or friendship can be an unforgivable transgression.

Being a boy kept me in a body that presented as androgynous, quirky, tomboy, singular. It was a queer body that created discomfort for the world, but my family, friends, and most of the people in my profession embraced it as the true me; they had accepted and counted on my queerness. The opposite happened when I became a man. The world scooped me up and gave me a warm welcome in places I could never before have entered comfortably, and many of the people closest to me turned away, betrayed by a transition they took personally.

My father soured me to the idea of manhood from the get-go. My wife of twenty years wasn't encouraging about the subject. She has identified as a lesbian for forty years, and though she loves boys, especially our nephews, men haven't been of particular interest to her. She never had any intention of living with one. And as much as I had done every single thing to look like a man and live like one, I denied wanting to become one because I didn't want to become my father or lose my lesbian lover or be a failed feminist and intellectual.

As a feminist for my entire adult life, and as someone who completed a PhD in cultural studies, my transition creates ripples of complications for my brain, a brain that lived with certainty about the elasticity of gender and its capacity to flex and expand with the culture. I desperately wanted to inhabit my ambiguity as a political position, as a way to say that I would not perpetuate a binary that almost killed me, but when I heard the definitive nature of that "sir" inside the Hotel Chandler, my body never wanted to look back. I imagined myself packing a single bag, a change of clothes, my passport, and some cash, and boarding a plane to another country to live the life I had missed for whatever time I had left on this earth.

My head and my body were at odds. I had been scrutinizing masculinity my whole life, trying to perfectly replicate it in my gestures and clothes and physique. I stayed very trim, wore only men's clothes, studied the latest short-hair styles, tried to keep the tenor of my voice low, and always played the roles that I thought men played. I earned. I mowed the lawn. I kept track of the finances. I filed the taxes. I shoveled the snow. I lugged the air conditioners from the basement to the bedroom windows every summer. I always drove. I was grossly deficient at housecleaning. I owned only one bathroom towel when my wife, Lynette, first moved into my bachelor pad. But I insisted that I was not a man, until at age fifty, the knowledge that I had only ever felt like a man and a boy poured out of me with a certainty that I would never deny again. I learned quickly that it's okay to theorize about bodies, but altering a body's sex is perhaps the greatest disruption to the social order that makes up friendship, work, and love.

My body's biological need is to live as a man. It presents a gender theory problem. My PhD had trained me to put all of my emphasis on the cultural manifestations of gender as a construct. I see queer and trans people wearing T-shirts now that read "Gender Is a Social Construct." I think the over-simplification of that is as dangerous as is the reinforcing of genitalia defining sex as God's will. A construct is something we make; it is a materiality that is drawn from the offerings of culture and reinscribed so seamlessly that it feels natural. For me, living as a woman was a construct. I am not a philosopher and this book is not a treatise on the ontological nature of being. What I know is that this transition wasn't something I knew I wanted, it wasn't something I chose. It was a long-ing and a desire so deeply embedded in my body that I could barely access it because every part of my life, all that culture had to offer, told me I couldn't have it. I believe my maleness is the truest and most stable thing about me, and has been so since my earliest memories. I experience myself as a man; not as a construct, but how I construct that man knowing what I know as a woman is my work now.

There is a photo of me at age four with my older brother and some of my cousins. I'm wearing my brother Tim's purple paisley shirt, an article of clothing I adored; it's unbuttoned and my naked chest is sticking out proudly and I have a huge smile on my face. That boy knew who he was. How the culture of my childhood and most of my adulthood made living and exploring that truth both impossible and deadly is the trauma that formed my emotional core, separated my soul from my living, breathing existence. My body could feel alive and my heart could feel warm only when testosterone reunited me with that boy at age four who, I so clearly remember, dreamed of being a man.

"That's what she wanted. White picket fences. Happy hubby, romantic, man and woman. And yet, she had the body she had, and she was who she was."

These are the words of the best friend of the first transgender person killed in the United States in 2018. Christa Leigh Steele-Knudslien was bludgeoned with a hammer by her husband and then stabbed in the back and through the heart. "She had the body she had." These six words play over and over again in my head. The inescapable doubling of the transgender body, expressed as if doubling means a life can never be complete, as if a certain combination of body parts is necessary to achieve "happiness," even for a best friend who knows which pronouns to use.

How to tell you what it feels like? How to bring you inside this experience with me, so that you can be not just open-hearted, but so you can know me, so that when I die, you can say the right words? Please don't say "he had the body he had." Please don't ask me if I feel incomplete because the top half doesn't match the bottom, as one good friend did. I love this body and all its contradictions. Please know that many things are true about my history that can never add up. I was conscripted to the girls' locker room and the women's restroom, but when I was speaking to you I was always speaking to you as the boy I was and the man I am. I knew I had to check the F box on my passport application to go to college in London, but when I saw the photos of me standing next to Windsor Castle, I didn't recognize her and turned away. I will always feel the rage of being a woman who was told on too many occasions that I was aggressive and ambitious and angry. I feel those feelings as her, even though she's me and not me. An inner self can learn to walk parallel with a constructed self and know and not know it simultaneously.

I am transgender to my past, to all the people who knew me as Polly. Friends will say, when I am not around, "You know, he was she before he was he." I will enter rooms where my past is present and watch people search for the woman in me. I am an object of curiosity in one setting and the embodiment of privilege as I flaunt my whiteness and masculinity in another. I am a spy. I watch men and how they behave: I am at the pool. A man dismisses a young woman's kind request. She has reserved the lane he is in for the lesson she will teach, the schedule posted on the door to the entry to the pool. "This is my lane." He sneers at her and swims on. The next time he pops his head out of the water I shout at him, "Move the fuck over, buddy," and he does. My body is at risk as trans and it has incredible mobility as white and male. I represent a threat to the lone woman walking in the park with her dog, and I am perhaps the greatest hope for the young trans students at the college where I teach, the only transgender professor as of this writing.

I have never felt so much. I am like a newborn who is expected to drive sixty-five miles per hour down the highway, but I can't see above the steering wheel. I crane my neck upward to get a glimpse of wholeness in the rearview mirror and weep with relief at that gorgeous gray-haired man. I want to believe that my past is behind me, that I will look at him forever, that we are undivided. There is an episode in the Amazon television series *Transparent* in which the trans women on the show have their childhood photos altered to reinvent their history, to imagine their pasts different from what they were, to see themselves as the young girls they wish they had been. I want this, too, at the beginning. But I am a married man, and this transition isn't singular. I was a lesbian lover once and now I am a husband. What to do with my history of loving the same woman for twenty years when both bodies worship the ground she walks on?

Old relationships formed under a dead name flounder, dead-ending, ending. "You changed," they say—all the ways of coming into being as a transgender person threaten the chronology of history and memories for others. "Be prepared to lose everything," my healthcare provider tells me when I start testosterone. This hardly feels like a warning because I think I can't lose everything fast enough. I want her to stop talking and just give me that testosterone shot. But she was right, and over the course of these two years I have to face the loss. It's taboo in the trans community to use someone's "dead name." Do not, for example, put a dead name in an obituary, or refer to the time when she was her if he is now him. I break that taboo in this book. You must know Polly, as much as I will begrudge telling you, because Polly knows so much about Carl and vice versa.

Polly knows what it is to be treated as a woman and to live inside the confines of the female gender. Carl knows the freedom of being a man and what happens in spaces where only men are allowed to go. Polly felt intensely the discrimination of being a successful woman, a leader in American theater. Carl witnesses the discrimination against women everywhere now in a way that Polly's body couldn't take in. I am a work in progress, always doubling as different selves in different spaces, still learning how to navigate the multiple truths this body inhabits. When I shout at that man in the pool, it's Polly's memories and Carl's body.

I am slowly being surrounded by many young people who define themselves as nonbinary, friends who refuse to pick a side and use the pronoun "they." And this possibility, one that feels very recent, may change the gender landscape for the better. It is a different experience of being trans and one that I am eager to continue to learn from. At the same time, white masculinity is more defined and powerful than ever—in the workplace, in the government, in the gym where I work out every day, in my little apartment in Berlin where I watch Kavanaugh testify, shout in anger, cry out over the indignation of being held accountable, lie repeatedly, and then get sworn into a lifetime appointment to the Supreme Court.

I walk in the world as a man. I am experiencing that privilege for the very first time and I love it unapologetically. This side of the binary suits me. But I can't walk freely and act like I don't know what women face in a culture of men who dismiss a women's terror and traumas and history as unworthy of consideration. I will not recover from what I am seeing, a woman recounting her deepest pain in front of a group of disinterested and disbelieving men who run our country. The part of the assault most etched in Blasey Ford's memory, of two boys/men laughing, not at her, but with each other over their power to destroy her life. I know she did not forget who was in that room. As my visible queerness has dissipated, and the fog of being disassociated from my body has lifted, I see with crystalline clearness the power that operates in men's bodies—power that threatens the very integrity of our nation-state.

I see all the flaws of men, all the ways their fragility makes them dangerous and powerful and dismissive and sure that they know it all, and I love being a man. I love masculinity and I love hanging out with men. My body is a contradiction. I feel a fiery rage toward men for treating me like a woman, for making women seem crazy and emotional and inferior, for what men did to me. I feel so much joy living in a man's body, my natural physicality, and I am trying to find a path toward becoming a good man.

If we are to survive America's current war over who gets to have a livable life, we must confront and understand masculinity and we must all seek some version of double consciousness, to be inside and outside of identities that are not our own. Transgender people have something important to offer this conversation, and perhaps if we are allowed to speak, if we're heard, we too will have a chance at more livable lives.

CHAPTER TWO

LOSING HER

BOSTON, MASSACHUSETTS

> Some time later there was a song on all the jukeboxes on the Upper East Side that went "but where is the schoolgirl who used to be me . . ."
> —Joan Didion, "Goodbye to All That"

Friday I will go home for the first time as my mother's son. It is a Monday in September of 2017, and I'm trying to figure out how to stay alive until I board a plane from Boston to Elkhart, Indiana, my hometown. I make a list in my little blue notepad to soothe myself:

Shaving cream in a deep lather on my face
The blue of the pool at the gym
The bench press
The smell of my hair pomade that I got at a barbershop
    named Virile

My monthly subscription to men's grooming products
*   that comes in a fancy box*
My barber, Stephen
A list of bourbons I love: Nikka, Widow Jane, Elijah
*   Craig, Larceny*
Noah, the bartender
Alex, my swim coach
Sonny, an athletic man's dog

My mother has "predementia." I don't know exactly what that means. I know that she was at the emergency room last Sunday for diverticulitis and didn't remember that she had been there three weeks earlier for vertigo. I don't know if she remembers that we were best friends once, that I called her every day of my freshman year of college even though I was only twenty minutes from home. I don't know if she remembers that visit to Minneapolis at the behest of my therapist. I was thirty years old and had been diagnosed as bipolar and was struggling with suicidal thoughts. In the session, she told the therapist and me, "You've been acting like my mother for too long, and now I'll be the mom, and it's my time to have my own life." Does she remember leaving me then? For good? I don't know if she knows I'm her son now. What is the difference between memories lost to disease and memories lost to shame and grief?

I am at my dining room table at 4:30 P.M. drinking a Leffe, a Belgian beer I like a lot. I have a slight buzz. I have been listening to Stevie Nicks's "Landslide" on repeat for hours:

Well, I've been afraid of changin'
'Cause I've built my life around you
But time makes you bolder

This morning at the gym I was standing with a towel around my waist, shaving in front of the mirror, cleaning up around my beard, when a fiftyish white guy, tan, wearing a peace symbol on a chain around his neck, came up behind me to tell me how awesome my chest tattoo looked. I have a red-tailed hawk soaring across my pecs, right underneath my nipples, which covers the scars from my top surgery, a double mastectomy in laywoman's terms. There was shaving cream all over my face and we stopped and talked tattoos for a bit. He was getting his first one next week. Over his left shoulder would be the handprint of his new grandson. I told him I used to walk along the Mississippi River every morning and would see the red-tailed hawks swooping overhead. "Such powerful birds," I said. It was a pleasant and simple exchange. I absorb locker room talk into the pores of every inch of my skin. I love hanging with men, and I love empty banter with men, and I love being a man. I don't want to leave the gym.

Well, I've been afraid of changin'
'Cause I've built my life around you
But time makes you bolder
Even children get older
And I'm getting older, too
Oh, I'm getting older, too

I am getting older. Like my mother, who got her master's in social work at age fifty-five, I have become a man at fifty-one. My parents haven't seen this man, his beard and his swagger. They know from my brothers and social media that I live as a man now. My mother still calls me Polly Precious and Sweet Pea, and my dad, who isn't predementia, calls me P or rather, "P, Pol, I mean P, Polly, I mean P." No one in my family can call me Carl.

When I think about going home, I know I am already dead. I think of my life as a daughter and a sister, the only girl. Daughters take care of things. They make sure their brothers remember their parents' birthdays and anniversaries. They help shop for and cook the holiday meals. They coordinate Dad's fiftieth birthday party. I was never a girl or a woman, but I was always a very good daughter and sister. I was/am my parents' favorite—a complicated and strange distinction. My dad hated me in most respects as a mouthy woman, but he knew as his only girl that I would step up and into whatever was needed to take care of him and my mom. In my parents' conventional world, daughters do the caretaking, no matter the circumstances. My brothers, with relief, always referred to me as the "glue" that held the family together. I sent my parents five hundred dollars every Christmas because I knew they were broke; my brothers sent them pictures of their children. Brothers get to enact a certain and expected obliviousness. Being a daughter means being as tired as all the men in the family after a huge Thanksgiving dinner, but doing the dishes with Mom. Being a daughter, even in the most masculine iteration pretransition, means your mother still refers to you as "her beauty queen." I want to convince myself that I can live as Polly in Elkhart and Carl everywhere else. After all, nobody cares what happens in Elkhart, Indiana—a small-minded and depressing little town where my mother is considered its most gay-friendly therapist because she once had a lesbian daughter.

But Polly's disappearance isn't just an Elkhart problem. A former best friend writes me a long email with the subject line "Putting Our Friendship to Rest." She and I haven't talked since I started testosterone but she lets me know that my temperament has changed, and her email complains that the way I transitioned was disrespectful to our friendship, that she had a "girlfriend named Polly," and I needed to better prepare friends for losing her.

When I first started talking about taking testosterone, I was mid-sentence in my therapist's office: "Well when I made the choice to have my breasts removed—" She interrupted me immediately, "Choice? Choice? What? Carl," she said, leaning forward in her small green velvet chair and chopping at the air emphatically, "choice is deciding whether to have kale salad or a BLT for lunch." I knew immediately in my body what she was saying. It is a failure of language, the reason that a woman's right to "choose" an abortion continues to be mis-articulated as a "choice." This word with no context, without a memoir to explain it, suggests an unconstrained free will. I choose to inject testosterone into my thigh every two weeks; no one straps me to a table and plunges a needle into my leg, but nothing about any stage of my transition feels like choosing between kale salad and a BLT.

Transphobia isn't simply a fear of transgender people, or a misunderstanding of the interactions between nature and culture; it is the inability to inhabit what another body feels and properly link those feelings to thoughts and words. One night I text my therapist, "I wish I could find the right language to describe what my body feels now, to make people understand." She texts back, "Much of being alive is wordless. It is embodied and acted out. It is a story told through behaviors and relationships." But this takes time, I think to myself. I don't know if I have any more time.

In January of 2013, I received an email from the human resources department at the college where I teach saying that gender confirmation surgeries would be covered by our health insurance. I remember forwarding the email to Lynette, asking "Please let me do this." Lynette hadn't wanted to lose these parts of Polly, but I had been trying to convince her for years that I needed this surgery, and this time she agreed to support me, feeling my desperation, knowing we could afford to do it now. The next thing I remember is waking up with a huge white bandage around my chest and a tube draining blood from each side of me where my breasts used to be. I don't remember choosing anything, certainly not a plan for my transition. At the time, I promised Lynette, "Just top surgery, never hormones." No wonder she's so angry now; it's more loss than she can bear. But I wasn't lying then. I didn't know. Doors opened and I fell through them. There was no plan, no choosing, just surviving from one moment of the transition to the next—top surgery, pronoun change, name change, hormones, white man. I never thought about losing her, just finding him.

Choice is the correct word for my decision not to think about my parents during this transition. I haven't seen my parents since my fiftieth birthday party in Minneapolis. I had just changed my pronouns to "he" and "him," and every exchange of words with *everyone* became fraught with missteps and apologies and discomfort. As much as I had hoped I could call myself he and suddenly he would be visible, this didn't happen. I hadn't invited my parents to the party because I couldn't deal with "him" and them, but they showed up anyway. They were hard to manage—my father constantly fretting about timing his diabetes shot and when we would eat, my mom upset that my older brother, whose house they were staying at, didn't stock her cranberry juice and ginger ale in his refrigerator. I think the predementia was already in motion. My mom seemed frustrated and out of her element, unable to understand we were hosting a party and she didn't have to worry about splitting the bill at the restaurant. But the strangeness had been this way between my mom and me for so long, I didn't recognize her vacancy and confusion as new. When she left me twenty years ago, she started talking in clichés. "Are your ears ringing? They should be, I was telling one of my clients about you today." This is her opening line every time we speak. When she was in her forties and I was an undergraduate, I encouraged her to go back to school. She had dropped out at nineteen to marry, like many women of her generation. I spent part of my college years helping her write papers, as she double-majored in women's studies and psychology. "You told me to get a life and I wouldn't be who

I am today without you," she'd say like a robocall, the exact same sentences strung together for twenty years, every single phone call. I was her daughter when I told her to "get a life," a daughter desperately loyal to her mother. Where did that schoolgirl go?

After age four, my body split. I lived two distinct lives. I aspired to everything my brothers had—little plastic green army men and tanks, short hair, little bow ties for dress up, Boy Scout uniforms, a bike with a crossbar, freedom to cannonball off the diving board in swim trunks. But I lived as my mother's daughter. She made all of my clothes—a white lace First Communion dress with a blue ribbon belt, a yellow frilled jacket over a long sheer flower skirt for sophomore prom, another white lace dress, this time with a red ribbon belt, for junior prom. I stood anxiously as she hemmed and stitched me up year after year. My two selves walked side by side. I couldn't escape being her daughter. Some parts of me didn't want to.

I lived most of my life in a depressed darkness—a hyperintellectual head attached to a neurotic body. My mind always feels male. I talk with the frightening conviction of a man, and am described as angry, brilliant, intimidating. My perception of myself is completely out of sync with what people see. My body thought people knew I was a man. I only know now, after this year on testosterone, that people thought they were talking to a woman. Is this what "gender dysphoria" means—the clinical diagnosis of a trans body? My wife told me one morning before I left for work to write STFU (Shut the Fuck Up) on my hand, a strategy to say less—to appear less threatening. My body is all nerves—the energy it takes to hold a body together when all the structural surfaces have been cut through. The neurons that connect legs to torso to neck to head short-circuit—parallel lines that will never meet, until the universe bends and at fifty-one, the lines miraculously touch and the neurons sense each other again.

With every testosterone shot I feel myself reconnecting to that boy, my mother's son. How to describe this to you? My body takes in emotions now, so when my wife says she loves me, I feel something travel across my skin into my pores and through my veins and around the ventricles of my heart and into the bones of my toes. These are feelings I have never had before. A body and a head in conversation with each other for the first time. The joy of being in the right locker room, the barber's chair. My hand rubs my beard and I look down at the hawk soaring across my chest. Why would anyone insist on mourning Polly? The joy of knowing you can finally see what I have always felt is a euphoria I never want to let go.

People of color and women and queers and trans folks all know what it means to double, how to perform two different versions of themselves depending on the context. Women know how to comport themselves in meetings with powerful men. Brilliant women double as submissive and calm even though they are powerful and mad as hell. Black women let white women touch their hair so as not to create a stir. Doubling is a survival tactic. It is knowing that you are a self both separate from your gender and your skin color and your country of origin, and that you are always seen in the context of the histories that come with these descriptors. In what is proving to be an often violent turn of events, white men must double now too for the first time in our history, their bodies finally called out as subject positions with the kind of ruthless regularity that the rest of us already know. A white male journalist recently tweeted that it's a mistake for women to talk about white men as if they mean "all white men." White men can't bear to double. The utter disbelief that they too could be threatened in their conviction that they have always been whole, dominant, unchallenged, and singular is the rupture that has America in a deadly landslide.

My mother tells my father who tells my brother who tells me that she knows I am transgender but that I will always be her daughter, Polly. I already know when I walk into their home in Elkhart, Indiana, we will kiss like nothing has changed; to acknowledge the change would require my parents to look at me. My mother would have to shut off the recording in her mind, the memory of the daughter who saved her life once by helping her find a career and a purpose. My father would have to notice someone other than himself. In this way, they will be like Lynette and many of my friends, people I've known for years who say nothing about my physical transformation. It's like I have gone from 400 pounds to 160 pounds and the people closest to me, and people I have known all of my life, will not allow me the kindness of noticing. It's a silent cruelty that screams judgment. The silent cruelty followed by straight-up transphobia: "I hope he gets what he wants out of this; he's just going to be a tiny little man, and they have no power." "He's overly sensitive now." "He's more aggressive." "He's changed." This transphobia is unexpected, especially from my liberal circle of colleagues and friends, but it's overt and clear and raises important questions. What parts of bodies are allowed to change without causing disruption? What are the qualities of sex and gender that make friendships? How do facial hair and broader shoulders disrupt human connection and sexual desire? How is a daughter different from a son?

I relish all the places where people only know me as Carl. I relish every exchange as the man I am. I want to be in a perpetual present tense. Judith Butler says that our future as a country depends upon knowing we are all living precarious lives, that my "I" is "bound to the subject that I am not."

That our reliance on one another determines if we will live, thrive, or die. But what about reliance on a body that was never mine? Can she and I ever untangle? I can no longer be bound to my parents and to her and still live. Who is a trans person bound to? Am I bound to my past or my present?

And if you see my reflection in the snow-covered hills
Well the landslide will bring it down
Oh, the landslide will bring it down

———————

Am I indulging the worst kind of man's journey? Am I gorging on every white American male fantasy to be his rugged individual self? To have a midlife crisis and leave his family behind for beer and bourbon and swim lessons? Am I killing off Polly to escape what she knows, the pain she endured? Worse, does becoming a man require unknowing at a visceral level what men do to women?

My therapist is teaching me about what connection to a body feels like and how that feeling can translate to others. First I feel me alive and then I feel others alive and then I feel others feel me alive. It's a process of reintegrating a person cut into parts. My problem has been dissociation, in therapy speak. "Wholeness isn't selfish," she tells me, "you don't have to decide between your 'I' and others," but the "we" of connection only comes when I have an "I." This sounds like a cliché that my mother might speak.

I am terrified that going home will be the landslide that will upend this forward motion toward me, toward my cliché of an "I" that has no idea how to incorporate all the knowing of that schoolgirl who used to be me.

I had an anxiety nap yesterday. I was sound asleep on the couch at about 3 P.M. and I dreamt I was running in a tight T-shirt and pair of shorts. I could feel my legs carrying me easily as I ran faster and faster, until I came to a set of stairs, and, without slowing, tumbled down them into an abyss. Not hard to translate. Elkhart is the abyss. How does a trans man make it out of the recreational vehicle capital of the world and actually live this long?

> Well, I've been afraid of changin'
> 'Cause I've built my life around you
> But time makes you bolder

What is possible for my relationships in this transition? If I'm not my mom's Polly Precious, what can we be to each other? If I'm not the daughter ready to step in and care for my parents in their old age, what kind of son can I be?

CHAPTER THREE

WESTERNS AND WAR

ELKHART, INDIANA

Only now is the child finally divested of all that he has been. His origins are become remote as his destiny and not again in all the world's turning will there be terrains so wild and barbarous to try whether the stuff of creation may be shaped to a man's will or whether his own heart is another kind of clay.
—Cormac McCarthy, *Blood Meridian: Or the Evening Redness in the West*

I've watched at least five westerns a week for the past sixteen years.
—My father

THE GOOD, THE BAD AND THE UGLY

I grew up on a steady stream of westerns in Elkhart, Indiana. At my house, it was never too early for a western—the ultimate white male fantasy. I would be lying in bed at 6 A.M. and hear the television blaring—some shoot-out from the

O.K. Corral. My dad is obsessed with them. He has likely seen every western ever made at least ten times. When I was visiting my parents in 2014 and my wife and I were trying to head back to Boston after having spent three days in the glow of tumbleweeds and bullets, I could hear from the back bedroom, at 6:45 A.M.: "Pol, Pol, Pol, Pol, Pol." My dad needed me urgently. "Pol, this is hands down the best duel in all of western history, you gotta watch this." He's actually right—it's the three-way duel from the end of *The Good, the Bad and the Ugly*. After years of watching Sergio Leone's spaghetti westerns, I can't help being drawn into this five-minute scene even if I haven't had my coffee yet. You have to remember the Ennio Morricone soundtrack that opens the film, that distorted whistle, that perfect sense that you are in the wild where there are no laws, that danger lurks behind every swinging saloon door. The duel is one of the best cinematic moments in film history. There they are, Clint Eastwood—the Good; Lee Van Cleef—the Bad; and Eli Wallach—the Ugly; in the middle of the most barren, cracked landscape in all of the country, where there's been no rain for at least thirty years, standing atop the rocky ground in the middle of a cemetery. They are in a wide circle, and they spend at least four minutes of the scene looking from side to side as the camera pans from eyes to hands on guns to angles of all three in shooting range of one another. Wallach is ugly because he has weird eyes, and they bobble around in his head throughout the whole scene. Van Cleef is bad because he's missing the tip of his middle finger on his shooting hand, as the camera shows us several times. Clint Eastwood is good because he is blond; they call him Blondie, and he is pretty, even when sweaty and dirty. My favorite part is when Eastwood finally pulls the trigger and knocks Van Cleef down, and Van Cleef tries to get up and shoot Eastwood. Eastwood delivers the final bullet, and Van Cleef rolls into an open grave, now his grave. The bad bury themselves.

I'M A BOY I'M INVISIBLE

I was a boy with two brothers, an older brother age six and a younger brother just born. My parents still have a picture of me blown up to twelve by eighteen sitting in the corner of their TV room, which they rarely leave. The photo is from May 10, 1969, my third birthday, and I am modeling my gifts, the only time my parents got me exactly what I asked for. I'm wearing yellow pants, a white shirt, a holster with a toy gun, cowboy boots, spurs, and a cowboy hat, and I look utterly joyful. I was already inhabiting my own western fantasy.

Christmas Eve, 1969. The tree has presents stacked around it. My grandfather, my father's father, is a talker and a boaster, and he can't wait to point out that the biggest present under the tree is mine. I'm beside myself. I'm trying to peel the edges of the wrapping paper from the box. I'm showing my cousins how much bigger my box is than theirs. When I finally open the box, I see it's a doll. A giant doll. She has brown hair, blue plastic eyes with a heroin gaze, pinkish white rubbery skin, and she is wearing a white dress with pink flowers and a little white and pink sweater that my grandmother crocheted for her. I'm three. Rage rushes up from my feet, my cheeks turn red, and there's a photo that captures me holding that doll, flush from disappointment with a look of fury on my face. I want to go home now. I can't fathom how they got it so wrong. I hate dolls. My mother liked the doll, though. She kept it for me and to this day it sits in a little doll rocking chair in the room I sleep in whenever I'm in Elkhart.

I know I'm a boy. Everyone sees a girl. Nothing I say can convince anyone otherwise. Nobody can see me. I am invisible.

I want G.I. Joes for my birthday. I love everything connected to war: the camouflage uniforms, the plastic cannons, and the green jeeps with thick tires. I want the red-headed G.I. Joe who has the full red beard. I'm obsessed with him. It's what I imagine myself looking like when I'm older; even though I don't have red hair, he makes me wish I did. I get a Barbie DreamCamper van. I never wanted a Barbie. Why can't I just have the G.I. Joes I said I wanted? These little deaths, misrecognitions that come with years of the wrong gifts and the wrong clothes, upend the becoming of a young trans body. Bendable plastic skinny Barbie sits in a pink van in my bedroom. She has a pink bikini outfit with matching pink heels for the beach and blue cropped sequin pants and a halter for everyday wear. The Barbie tragedy has a rare happy ending. Troy lives down the street from me and he covets girls' toys. He begged me for my Easy-Bake Oven the previous summer until I finally gave it to him so he could bake little cakes and sell them for ten cents. He wants that Barbie camper van, and he has two G.I. Joes that just lie on his bedroom floor untouched, the red-headed one and another with dark hair and a full beard. We make an epic and life-saving trade for both of us.

The girls in junior high torture me for not being like them. They tell me I'm in the wrong bathroom and mock my tomboy style. "You look like a boy, your hair's too short," they hiss behind my back. My girl cousins stop inviting me to their slumber parties. I don't care about makeup, or kissing boys, or clothes, or—I don't even know what else to include on the list. What do girls in junior high even like to do? It's not that I have no interest in being a girl, it's that I'm not one and can't connect to the experience in any way. I am fully formed in my otherness by the time I am twelve years old.

This alienation leads to a rage that I will carry with me my whole life. The rage becomes another way that I am two people. I am mad at everyone—my parents for not seeing that I'm not a girl, the girls at school for actually seeing that I'm not a girl, the boys for not recognizing I am one of them. This rage lives next to the good girl who is eager to please, my straight As, my intellectual curiosity, my love of animals, my political passion for justice. I am the top student in my class when in my seventh-grade art class I tell Mrs. Sinclair, the sweet, round, blonde arts and crafts teacher to *fuck off*. I smoke pot on the playground with three other boys. I'm kicked out of St. Thomas Catholic School for my transgressions. I'm so fucking angry. I start to masturbate to a fantasy about my death. It's a car accident. As the doctors try to stanch the bleeding, I am hooked up to all kinds of machines; I won't make it, and I orgasm when I die. Relief is my body lifeless and flatlining. I am kind of an antihero like Cormac McCarthy's "kid" in *Blood Meridian*, who is born with a penchant for bloodshed and violence, who travels across Texas killing as he goes. For me the violence is manifested inside the turmoil of my body; the harm I seek is to myself and my violent travels are mostly in my imagination, except when they leak out in the furious fucks of scary temper tantrums maybe only hours before I accept my award as the tennis team's Most Valuable Player or receive my recognition as my high school's valedictorian.

I am a good girl and I am angry and lethal. When I am eighteen, I take a job as a teller in a bank to make money for college. I have to wear pantyhose and skirts every single day. This job pays $8.25 an hour. The fast food jobs in Elkhart pay $5.00, minimum wage, but at least I could have worn jeans. I need the money. Money and ego drive westerns and war and I don't have either, though I desperately want both. If only I could rob the fucking bank. Touching people's money, looking up their depleted accounts and telling them I can't cash their checks because of NSF, nonsufficient funds, is almost like shooting them in the face. Men yell at me constantly for being the bearer of the news of their own possible demise. How do I defend myself from their rage dressed like a girl, a light covering of makeup on my face that my mother insists upon before I walk out the door each morning? I want to punch men long before I become a man, but I smile like a girl is supposed to and tell those nasty men, "Have a nice day."

After I finish my master's degree in peace studies at the age of twenty-four, I go to Florida to work with the Catholic Church, to develop a social justice curriculum and run a youth group for migrant farmworkers from Mexico. The conditions in Deland, Florida, are as harsh as any western. Generations of families are jammed into small trailers, some without running water; food and money are scarce, poverty is backbreaking, the kids in their early teens and their parents work fifteen-hour days in the fields picking ferns—the greenery that gets added to floral bouquets we send via FTD. Bodies get destroyed by their thirties or forties; this kind of labor isn't meant for any gender. I try to become good in that evangelical sense, to take what is bad and ugly in the world, and maybe make a dent in lives that are already predetermined. The families teach me to make tortillas and carne asada and barbacoa. I speak Spanish and wear dresses out of respect for the church and the traditions of the culture. I choose brightly patterned sundresses and Birkenstock sandals. Father Ted is my boss, a soft-spoken, gentle man who also speaks fluent Spanish. I think I want to be like him, to move in the world like a healer and an activist, a forgiver of sins. He never takes much interest in me, and the loneliness in Deland—no connection to myself and the despair over the circumstances of lives I cannot change, including my own— turns into a life-threatening depression. Father Ted, I learn a few years later, was a predator of a young beautiful blond boy; not unlike me, that boy was also trying to do something good in the world, looking to Father Ted as a mentor.

Nine months into the job, in the midst of a deadening and isolated depression, I drive my brand-new 1990 red Honda Civic into traffic on Colonial Drive in Orlando, Florida. My first suicide attempt. I wake up in the emergency room and I'm still alive. I am lying on a gurney in a neck brace with my sundress ripped from hip to ankle to tend to my bleeding and swollen knee. I can hear someone next to me throwing up but I am immobilized, like in my sexual fantasy; I am strapped tightly to a backboard, my heart racing at 140 beats per minute according to the EMT, even though I'm not moving. A local sheriff comes by and puts a ticket on my chest for a traffic violation. Like the men savoring the taste of blood and death in McCarthy's novel, this moment is my blood meridian; it permanently forms a flowing red circle that runs north to south across the poles of my body.

TERROR

You see, in this world there are two kinds of people, my friend: Those with loaded guns, and those who dig. You dig.

—Clint Eastwood as Blondie,
The Good, the Bad and the Ugly

When my therapist asks me for an image that describes what my body feels like, I tell her about the character Chris Taylor in the Vietnam War film *Platoon*. I think about his evolution as an innocent soldier with no experience to a state of hardened revenge at the end of the film, lying in a pile of dead bodies buried in mud and blood and body parts, and picking up a rifle to kill Sergeant Barnes, because justice tastes better than morality. I want justice, and I connect to being barely alive in a pile of bodies in a war zone of utter helplessness, in a war that will seemingly never end. But, I explain, I am also Major Winters from the HBO series *Band of Brothers*. He is a great leader of men, an amazing tactician and strategist. He always has a map and a plan. He lives in a state of hyperalertness, and this makes him an exemplary soldier. He survives World War II because of it. I'm a soldier on high alert and a survivor. I'm carrying matches, compass, bayonet, entrenching tool, ammunition, gas mask, musette bag with ammo, my .45 weapon, canteen, two cartons of smokes. My uniform is covered in mud and blood and even from a pile of dead bodies I will emerge to make my way to the next battle—some combo of Taylor and Winters—brains and maps and mud and rage.

Nine months after the Hotel Chandler I will have a kanji symbol that means soldier tattooed on my left wrist. I have lived a life in the bunkers of gender trauma that has been so brutal I know the fact that I am alive is a miracle. The only reality that my body can fully connect to is steeped in western showdowns at sunset, the beaches at Normandy in World War II—death, trauma, and survival stories that mirror those in the movies and history books I have been obsessed with my entire life.

Some statistics: In a report published by the National Center for Transgender Equality in early 2016, 40 percent of respondents, nearly nine times the national rate, had attempted suicide. In a 2017 report by the US Department of Veterans Affairs, the suicide rate among veterans was 22 percent higher than the general population, the bulk of that statistic being male. Transgender people and war veterans often give up on the idea of achieving a livable life. Trauma is the link between trans people and veterans, battering and unsustainable body trauma. My metaphors don't feel like metaphors.

In early October 2016, almost two months into taking testosterone, I call my therapist from Boston Common. It's a warm fall day. I'm not in a muggy rice paddy. I'm not in the hedgerows of enemy territory. I'm standing by a large white gazebo in the middle of the Common. People are riding bikes, pushing babies in strollers; tourists and students are taking photos; dogs, like dogs everywhere, are pulling leashes toward bold squirrels and pigeons. I don't remember what triggered it, I just know for certain I'm not going to make it. I can't breathe, my heart is racing, and my impulse is to step in front of traffic on Tremont Street, to splatter myself on the pavement to make the terror stop. On the phone, my therapist asks me to describe my surroundings and she says, "But do you feel like you're in a bunker? Does the Common feel like a war zone? Do you feel like a bomb could drop on you at any moment?" This is exactly it. I see for the first time that my mind knows I am on the Boston Common on a warm fall day, no threats anywhere near me, and my body feels itself to be somewhere else entirely. This is PTSD, my therapist tells me. I can't begin to describe the epiphany of that moment, to be able to understand that my body lives in a world of past traumas and they can surface anytime and anywhere, completely unconnected to the reality of present moments. My body has never been able to separate past from present, like when a car horn goes off and an army veteran ducks for cover. This is how I live. "Carl," she says, "our work is to get you out of that bunker."

I lived a double life of career, creativity, and success, and most days, in the back of my mind, I was planning my suicide. Art, a military veteran, describes what my body feels like to the psychologist Edward Tick in his book *War and the Soul*—there's Art and there's his soul that sits next to him. "It's like my twin," Art says. "It's like there's two of me wherever I go." His soul split from his body in battle. This is my story too. There has always been my body and me. They lived side by side but were never together—a good girl and a very angry boy or maybe a good boy and a very angry girl. I don't know yet.

As I begin to embody the masculinity of my fantasies, I feel closer to death for a time. My wife suggests to me that I am angrier because of the testosterone. This pisses me off and perhaps proves her point. She doesn't get it. I don't believe I feel angrier because of the testosterone. I've been angry as long as I can remember. The myth to an outsider is that I speak "I am transgender" and then I feel better. The early stages of transition for someone who identifies with clarity on the opposite side of the divide they were assigned can be the most difficult to survive. I couldn't wait another minute to be properly addressed and seen. The endless drag of these months was nearly impossible to bear. I bought an expensive razor with a red handle and a racing stripe an hour after my first testosterone shot. I would need to wait almost a year to use it. I was done waiting. I could not stand to hear "she," "her," "ma'am," or "miss" one more time.

I also didn't see the grief coming. This is the PTSD that starts to plague me in the transition, flashbacks that have me trapped in a bunker, convinced I'm going to die—all the memories of what was and all the imaginings of what could have been. If I had followed that four-year-old knowing, would I have become a man sooner? What kind of life might I have had? Why hadn't someone helped me sooner? I had so much therapy in the years leading up to my transition. Why hadn't one person ever looked at me and said, "Do you think perhaps your gender is an issue for you?" "Might you be transgender?" Of course, I'm too old for anyone to have asked me that, but still, why had I suffered so long with no proper care? My trauma, my PTSD, is not only gender-related; there is abuse, family trauma, and only in the transition, only in feeling alive in a body can I understand my history, can my body feel the multiple sources of its own terror.

I feel the regret, and the anger goes as deep as the regret. I worry I will be a cliché of a disappointed white man. Isn't this one of the threads defining the toxic politics of white masculinity in 2019? All those white men, and the women who love them, grieving over what they thought was meant only for them, a prosperous America where any white man could access his version of the American dream. I hear Marlon Brando in *On the Waterfront* in my head: "I coulda been a contender." I feel that grief over my lost life as a man, what I might have become had that boy gotten to be a boy. To believe in a slogan like "Make America Great Again" is to buy into the delusion that the possibilities for white masculinity are being stolen by immigrants coming over our border and threatened by women who tell the truth about their sexual assaults. To wear that red MAGA cap is to believe in the fantasy that when we were a whiter country, where women knew their place and men could be men, dreams could be made whole. White men shooting up bodies in churches and schools and movie theaters are living in the Old West or in the Iraqi desert, killing anyone they think stole their America from them. A trans person who transitions as late as I did has to contend with more than half a life missed feeling the physicality of a self. Would it have been better to not know? To keep living as Polly? I don't want to be another white guy filled with rage, but I am for a while. It's a trauma I will never fully recover from, but ultimately *you* have to know as you read this that I will only live if I transition.

I conjure a new death fantasy in these early months, congruent with my three-year-old self dressed in a cowboy suit. I start to do research about how to get a gun. I can drive to New Hampshire and purchase one the same day. They have state-run liquor outlets along the highway there too. I will walk into a bar. I will drink a bourbon neat. I will go to a Motel 6, a grimy, shitty motel room, and drink the bottle of bourbon I picked up along the way. I might even smoke a cigarette even though I hate cigarette smoke. In my blue J.Crew duffle bag that usually carries my workout clothes, I will have a loaded gun. It will look like that gun Clint Eastwood carries in *The Good, the Bad and the Ugly*—a wooden handle inlaid with a silver rattlesnake, and a long black barrel. In my western fantasy in my hotel room with my bourbon and Clint's gun up against my temple, I say goodbye in a fit of rage, pissed at all of you for never seeing me.

This new fantasy puts me to sleep at night. But when I wake up I will rub my hands over my stubble, take off my T-shirt, and flex my muscles. I will look in the mirror and feel my head connected to my body for these first months of my life as me, and I will keep going, to see what kind of man I might become.

CHAPTER FOUR

BECOMING ME, LEAVING YOU

AN AIRPLANE FROM LONDON TO BOSTON

Loving you whether, whether
Times are good or bad, happy or sad
—Al Green, "Let's Stay Together"

Dear Lynette,

This has been the worst year of our marriage. We have never been more alienated from each other. I have never felt so alone in the world as I do as I write this. I swear a year from now we will still be together. We will work this out between now and then.

My leaving us came without warning and strangely without intention. I was speaking my truth to you all along, as I knew it and when I knew it. I thought you knew everything I knew. I would never let you call me "woman." We joked together about not being a lesbian couple because it assumed something about us that wasn't true. Though the single happiest day of my life was our marriage in front of that very kind justice of the peace in Newton, Massachusetts. It was a relatively warm early October morning—October 3 to be exact, the same day of the same month Barack and Michelle Obama were married! The justice of the peace had invited us to her home and had started a fire in the fireplace so we could feel the warmth to match the love in our hearts. I wasn't focused on the "gay" part of marrying you, the person I had been with for fourteen years, the person who had taught me about love, connection, and family. I never thought we were marrying genders. Perhaps this was naive. I know the history of gay rights includes the struggle for gender sameness to comingle legally and without discrimination.

I never equated my transition, becoming me, with leaving you. I wasn't looking for someone else to love. I didn't think my gender would matter to you, and I didn't think I was leaving. I felt I was appearing in the relationship for the first time. But as we sat in couples' therapy with the wise, eighty-two-year-old Barbara and heard her say, "Polly has left, and she's not coming back, how do you feel about that?" I saw the look in your eyes when it came out of her mouth. It's a look I wish I didn't have in my memory: slack-faced, confused, tired, angry, and devastated.

Polly did leave.

We don't say her name anymore and we don't use her pronouns. Her breasts have been long gone, and her body almost completely disappeared. You show your therapist pictures from our wedding and then pictures from a year into the transition and she gasps and says, "I wouldn't recognize this as the same person." You feel affirmed. At first, it doesn't make sense to me. "It's still me," I insist to you. "I'm the same person inside." Am I trying to convince you or myself? But we both know that the changes aren't just to the surface. I walk in the world in an entirely different way. Polly hid her body. Polly was familiar. She ate less, she smelled different, she was bipolar, she was behind the scenes, she assumed she was often wrong, she liked to be home and alone. She never talked to salespeople, or waitstaff, or hairstylists, and she hated to go into the water. She was impatient but more patient with you.

I wonder as I write this what you miss most. Do you miss the female parts, the softer edges, my breasts, the voice that is still on your voicemail of your iPhone, the voice you refuse to erase as a way to remember her? Do you miss our history of shopping in the men's departments and your insistence on someone waiting on me? You never took any shit from those clerks who ignored me, who treated me like I had wandered into the wrong part of the store. Do you miss saying my name? Do you miss calling me "Pol"? Do you miss my narrow shoulders and my smooth face? Do you miss feeling queer sitting at restaurants and reaching for hands across the table to see who we could shock? Do you miss how it felt to spoon, soft flesh on soft flesh? Do you miss my ambition being embodied in womanhood? Do you miss the more uncertain me? Do you miss the me that could only connect to you because you were all I trusted?

Can you trust a man, Lynette? You haven't once in this year run your hands along my face. You make that funny grimace every time I ask you about the beard. Do you think if I shaved you would see Polly again? One thing we've had in common is our disdain for asshole white men. We love my white brothers. We adored your white father. We have some white male friends. But we've never had a white man in our bed. Neither of us expected that; even though my four-year-old self knew, Polly had no idea she would let Carl into her bed, next to you. You can barely touch me now. I sometimes grab your hands and rub them across my pecs, hoping that you will come to love them as much as I do. Will you? When will we know?

You call me your husband now. What are your expectations of a husband? Did your young lesbian self ever imagine uttering those words? I like to joke with you about being a "lesbian's lesbian." You were queer long before the rainbow flags flew as a sign of welcome in restaurants and bars. You were an underground queer, a hard-ass femme who twirled butches around your finger. You are writing a novel about living as a femme in the '80s. Can a lesbian fiction writer go straight? Is our marriage still valid? Did I trick you at the altar? That's how you must feel.

You have a new look on your face when we sit across our breakfast table in the mornings and drink our coffee with our computers open and try to talk about all of this. It's like a shock that never wears off, that's frozen in time, that is waiting for Polly's return. I try to think of things to say so that look will go away. Sometimes I talk and talk and talk to cover the silence. I've never said so much and so little. Your face makes me wonder if you can ever love Carl.

The other day you asked me after our first couples therapy session whether I was planning on finding a younger woman and starting a family. I was stunned.

Is this what you're thinking I'm thinking? I'm thinking about not killing myself because I fear that this me that is me that I love so much is a scourge to you and to my colleagues and to all the friends I have lost in this transition. Kids? And yet we know many men who left their wives at fifty and started over with younger women and new families. We can name at least a handful. Of course you're thinking this, this is what men at midlife do.

You are sixty-two and I am fifty-one. And I look younger now, like your son. It infuriates you when I tell people your age. I love older women. I always have. I see it as a source of pride that I snagged you. You are the most beautiful woman I have ever seen. You turn me on. When I met you and I was thirty-two and you were forty-three, you were Sophia Loren in that poster I bought that we hung in our first house together. Sophia advertising canned anchovies in the 1950s with a little rope belt around her waist and underarm hair exposed as she holds one of the cans over her head. We love that poster. We have moved it from home to home and city to city. You and I have had nineteen years of a life together. We buried both of your parents. You asked me to read your mother's eulogy because you thought you wouldn't be able to, though you had written it in perfect meter, your writing a gift to us all. But when you looked over at me, I burst into tears, so you read it instead without a quiver. You are the stronger one, more likely to survive if we don't. When we buried your father, I knew we would be together forever. He loved us so much as a couple. He was our father and we knew we could never separate, that honoring his memory was more important.

My family is so much more fractured, and you've managed to hold us all together. My brothers and I couldn't plan my parents fiftieth wedding anniversary, so you did—with love and attention to detail—a Cubs game at Wrigley Field because my parents have been watching Cubs baseball their whole lives, Chicago deep-dish pizza at an old Italian pizzeria, and the warmth that comes with anything you plan—because you learned about family when I never did. Did I betray our family? I wonder if that is what is behind that look of yours? Did I betray you? Did I cheat on you with a man?

Testosterone is a burden to a marriage. I missed menopause. I transitioned in a frenzy when I turned fifty because I knew menopause, becoming an older woman, would kill me, that menopause would shove my femaleness in my face in a way that would make me too sick to live. Do you resent that I shoved testosterone into my thigh instead and said fuck you to menopause? You're still on estrogen. You face the invisibility that every woman over fifty faces. It's when women disappear and men cheat. I work in an industry where there are few acting parts for women your age, your moment in our culture has passed according to about every cultural reference, and we have no children, so no grandchildren to turn our attention to. I am being seen as you feel yourself disappear.

You have not disappeared to me. The other day in a text you wrote, "You don't see me." I knew what you were saying. I have been so obsessed with seeing myself and feeling my body and swimming and sitting at bars and flexing the muscles in my chest and arms. Transition is nothing if not a narcissistic moment in time. I couldn't bear to look at myself and now that's all I can do. It must be maddening to watch. But I know you remember that I couldn't look before. I do see you, Lynette. I see you hurting. I see your anger. You said to me a year ago, "I thought we were at the point in our relationship where we would cruise to the end. How could you do this now?" I ask myself that. I didn't know, please believe me when I say I didn't know, that I was risking us when I walked through the door to manhood. I am just now understanding how stupid that was but it was me or you and I chose me. Can this be love? Isn't love choosing your spouse over yourself? I ask myself this every day. I ask my therapist this every day. Am I a selfish asshole? You call me an ass all the time now. Only a selfish asshole would do what I did. I know that's how it feels to you. I know if you were drowning in our beloved Mississippi River, I would jump in without hesitation and risk my life to save yours. So why didn't I choose you? This is why I think of dying so often. I think my dying might save you, though my therapist says it would destroy you. Would it? I don't know why I chose me. I have never chosen me before. My whole career is choosing to support others in what they do. I've relished contributing to our home and our life, giving what I earn to us and to you. I have always stepped in when someone needed anything.

I haven't known Carl that long. Maybe he is a selfish ass. I can't be certain. You, Lynette, are definitely taking a risk to stay with someone just being born. I remember when Susan, the girlfriend I bought my first house with, broke up with me. She had had several affairs. She was having a long-term affair with a woman when she finally left me. She never had a job. I bought the house we lived in, the car we drove, the food we ate. She was always disappearing and then coming home to beg for forgiveness and I would easily forgive. She'd had a rough life. Her father was abusive, beat her mother to a pulp. Susan was a recovering alcoholic, whip-smart but without confidence. I cared for her like an abandoned puppy. And when she left I thought I wouldn't make it. Why? She barely paid any attention to me, but I didn't have a body so I didn't need much. About the time I started to feel a little better from the shock of the breakup, she left a letter in my mailbox. I remember the relief when I saw it. I had hoped we would become friends. She had left without a word. There was no couples' counseling or even conversations and fights. She was just gone. I opened the letter, glad to see the familiarity of her handwriting. We wrote letters then, not emails. It said, "Dear Polly, I wanted to let you know that not only did I fall out of love with you during our four years together, I realized that you are not even someone I like. I thought you should know that." That's when I punched my hand through the bathroom door and overdosed on lithium.

This is what my body is waiting for. I'm waiting for

you to tell me that you don't even like me, let alone love me. The difference between then and now is that I'm starting to like me. I like what I see in the mirror. I like that my body can feel the sorrow and grief and joy of this transition. I like that I am risking everything to feel like I belong somewhere—next to this six-foot man on this cross-country flight back to Boston, talking about beer and basketball and writing this letter to you. I like walking around and meeting people. I like dressing like a dude. I love my beard and my buzzed head. I love that I haven't shaved in five days and there's stubble everywhere. I can't stop touching it as I type.

But most importantly, I love you, Lynette, no matter what happens to us. No matter where we are a year from now. No matter if you have written a letter to me telling me you don't like me anymore. This book is dedicated to you, to your resilience, your strength, your beauty.

Despite the terrible grief between us:

You raised our new labradoodle, Lenny. She is perfect and keeps love alive in our sad house.

You rescued our white-trash dog, Sonny. Living in a van, starving, and without a social grace, you saved him when you didn't know how to save us.

You grew two abundant garden plots and we ate beets, radishes, potatoes, cabbage, broccoli, beans, kale, and tomatoes together all summer, even if we didn't speak to each other across the patio table.

You became politically active, hosting neighborhood gatherings to write postcards to our politicians protesting changes in environmental policy, discrimination against transgender people, discrimination against Muslims, discrimination against Mexican immigrants, discrimination against all immigrants—hundreds of postcards—our communal anger soothed by your pots of chili, baked lasagna, grilled Italian sausage, and your famous fennel and orange salad.

You went by yourself to your best friend's daughter's wedding, without me, because of my knee, and you ironed tablecloths and put out place settings for a hundred people.

I see you, Lynette. I see that perfectly wrinkle-free sixty-two-year-old skin. I see the flesh around your midsection that is new in the last few years, which you try to hide from me. I see all the candy you eat, so much candy, more than the children eat. Good & Plenty boxes fill the recycling bin. I see those tender lips when they turn toward a smile, they still melt me even in our worst moments. I see how lonely you are in Boston. Is it Boston? Is it age? Is it transition? Is it that your father is gone? I see the woman I fell in love with—warm, generous to a fault, angry, talented, directionally challenged, and perfectly you.

I realize you no longer get to see the woman you fell in love with. Is this the impossibility? Can we make something new out of memories, and our Italian loyalty, and our wedding vows?

I swear to God I'm fighting for you and for us.

I love you, always.

Carl

CHAPTER FIVE

A PHOTO

SEATTLE, WASHINGTON

You must know that there is nothing higher and stronger and more wholesome and good for life in the future than some good memory, especially a memory of childhood, of home.

—Fyodor Dostoevsky, *The Brothers Karamazov*

I open my web browser and Facebook graces me with a memory of their choosing—a photo my brother posted a few years back of my mom, me, and my two brothers Easter Sunday, 1971.

The photo jumps out at me like it's been plugged into an electrical outlet. Sparks are coming off it and it's hot to the touch. It's a photo I have seen many times before, but not since taking testosterone, not since living in a body that feels everything all the time. The photo is faded. My mother is standing behind the three of us, her left hand on my left shoulder and right hand on my brother Tim's right shoulder, my younger brother Christian standing in the middle blocking my mother's legs, not even waist-high. I am five years old, which makes Tim eight and Christian two and a half. We are all dressed for the occasion. My mother is in a bright yellow coat and a navy dress with vertical white stripes and a wide white collar. Her long black Italian hair is swirled in a stylish bouffant updo, very Holly Golightly with an ethnic twist. I am wearing a dress, but it's covered by an Easter-egg-blue coat, and the aging photo barely shows the socks that come up just below my knees. Tim, in his little-boy green-checked suit jacket and white dress shirt, already has that sad look on his face that will accompany him in every one of our childhood photographs. Christian looks like a bleached-blond stuffed doll, too young to know what's coming.

This photo is one of a series of childhood photos of me where I have my fists raised. In this one, my face is part smile and part protest, which aptly describes how I will move in the world for another forty-five years after this photo is taken— trying to get along, live with what I've been given, and fight to be seen and felt in my life. I don't look like a boy in this photo the way I do in others. I look like my mother's only daughter. When I see the photo, a flood of images from my childhood rushes up from my feet, through my rock-hard thighs, and lodges right into that pressured space behind my eyes where

I have newly refurbished nerve endings. These nerve endings attach feelings to the images and press out tears as if they run the show that has become my life.

The cherry tree to my left just outside the frame of the photo is where I would lie on my back in a cradle of branches hidden by the pink blossoms and try to read my brother Tim's Hardy Boys mysteries.

Later there will be a basketball court behind where we're standing in the photo that my dad will have a friend install. I will play on it alone after school, well into the dark every day when it's not pouring down rain or there isn't snow on the ground. I will make up opponents in my head, and sink last-second shots just before the buzzer for the win. I will learn to dribble on gravel, never able to predict which direction the ball will bounce, because we couldn't afford to pave the driveway. I learn ball control and become a first-rate point guard in high school.

Mr. and Mrs. Sommers's white garage is outside the frame, opposite the cherry tree. They were an older couple who yelled when our football went into their yard or a baseball smacked the side of the garage wall. They also opened their porch to us as a refuge when the fights between my parents felt like too much—when my mother threw all my father's clothes on the front lawn, or locked herself in the bathroom and threatened suicide.

Just north of where we're standing in the photo is a cement pad outside our back door. My dad loved toy poodles, and though he was never around to care for them, we had two growing up, Max and Benny. We would tie them to the corner of the cement pad on a long chain-link leash.

Before my mom puts her hair in that public updo that we see in the photo, I remember all the times we would stand in the tiny bathroom our family of five shared when she would allow me to touch her long black hair, free flowing while she unpinned her rollers that kept the frizzy curls straight and smooth. I was awed by this hair, its length, its fullness, as it cascaded over her shoulders for those few moments.

Today I feel this picture for the first time. It's nostalgia, in part, and I know in my head that nostalgia is problematic. It is the emotion of forgetting. It is why "Make America Great Again" is the biggest political lie ever perpetrated on the American people. If we went back—to no civil rights, no women's rights, no gay rights—we could move forward. But looking at this photo marks the first time since transitioning that I feel something soften in me about the past, about my mom. Nothing has felt soft about the work of excavating my childhood, sorting out gender trauma and family trauma, grieving what I missed.

DEMENTIA

Last week my brother Tim called me. He was upset. He had talked to my parents, something he rarely does. He has two boys, Max and Michael. Tim talked to my dad, then my dad handed the phone to my mother and she talked to Max, and then Max handed the phone to Tim and my mom thought she was talking to my younger brother, Christian. In other words, she had forgotten who Max belonged to.

I got off the phone and I had no idea how to feel. My mother has significant hearing loss. Her father, who had come from Italy and was in his eighties when I knew him, was almost completely deaf. As kids we always joked that Mom's hearing loss was selective. For example, one time when she was standing in the kitchen and I was walking downstairs to the basement, I muttered "go to hell," and she immediately replied, "I heard that." But talking to her on the phone over the years has become increasingly difficult as her hearing deteriorates. I wondered if it was the dementia or her hearing or some combination when she didn't know which son was on the phone. Or perhaps I don't know how to breathe in the possibilities of her deterioration, loss upon loss.

The night before Tim's call, I had told her that Lynette and I were coming to see her in a month. She immediately went to get her calendar to make sure she wrote the dates down and said, "Oh, it's already written on my calendar, 'the girls are coming.'" I don't expect her to remember that I am a man at this point; she's only seen me once as her son, and even if she didn't have dementia I'm not sure she would have allowed herself to register it. But the state of her hearing or emotional resistance aside, my mother's memory is definitely fading, and mine is taking over my body.

In the photo her thick and silky long black hair, which is now short and gray and fine, felt like it was brushing up against my fingertips. That hair terrified me and soothed me, much like she did. Once one of my cousins was over and saw my mom with her hair down and said she looked like a witch. I knew what she meant, though her saying so made me mad. When I was ten years old, I spilled a completely full glass of milk all over the kitchen table and my mother flew into her Calabrian rage, pulled out a wooden spoon from the drawer, and broke it over my behind, breaking a fingernail to the quick in the process. She always kept her fingernails long and perfectly polished. Every Saturday I would watch her sand them with an oversized emery board and then paint them, in bright red if there was a wedding or a party that weekend, and neutral shades for the rest of the week. I liked to help her pick out the colors, but on the few occasions when she asked if I wanted my nails painted, I said no. This morning, as the milk ran down the sides of the table and onto the floor, the polished nail on her right index finger snapped right off. I remember seeing the blood start to form around the cuticle, and I knew I was in huge trouble. Her pain intensified the rage. She furiously grabbed a brown paper grocery bag, ran back to my bedroom, flung open my dresser drawers, and packed underwear, socks, T-shirts, pajamas, and jeans. She shoved the paper bag at me, pushed me down the hall from behind and out the back screen door, walked me down the two cement steps and onto the cement pad to the sidewalk that led to the alley, and screamed, "Don't you ever come back!"

I remember every detail of the warm rain falling onto the brown bag on a humid summer day, softening the paper so the bag started to tear, my clothes poking through, me in my favorite red shorts with white stripes up each thigh and an orange T-shirt that I wore as often as I could get away with it. I held the bag and stood on the cement sidewalk. I had no idea which way to go.

This new body of mine feels the emotional and physical neglect in neon, at broken angles, in the well-worn cracks of an old sidewalk that led to a dilapidated garage and a gravel driveway.

I sometimes wonder if my mother's memory is disappearing as a way of not feeling things anymore. Not feeling the loss of her children, who come to visit only for obligatory holidays. Not feeling her own lack of effort to know her grandchildren. Not feeling the mourning of a daughter lost. I know I don't understand the science of dementia, and perhaps it has nothing to do with emotions, but her decline became visible as Polly disappeared. I am not blaming the transition, just wondering what tethers a mind to reality.

As I keep looking at the photo of us, I feel close to her for the first time in a very long while. What is that feeling? I am learning to wait to feel. Before having my own body, feelings would drown me. All feelings felt the same. Happy was confused with fearful and pain was confused with relief and sadness was confused with anger.

Today I am parsing feelings and letting them have their space. They will consume my morning coffee ritual, my ninety-minute workout, my writing time that doesn't include putting any words on the page. I remember a shopping trip to the Pierre Moran Mall in Elkhart before entering the eighth grade, when I would attend West Side Junior High, a public school, for the first time. My mom took me to the mall, a girls' afternoon out. She had no money to spend on me, and she had been so angry with me for getting kicked out of a private school, her Catholicism still devout, but she desperately wanted me to feel good starting a new school. She let me get a pair of maroon corduroy Levi's. Something that I liked, not something she thought I should wear. She let me put a blue-and-white-striped "boyish" shirt and a maroon V-neck sweater with a bold blue stripe across the chest on layaway. She promised she would chip away at paying it down so I would have the whole outfit by the time school photos were taken. I still have that photo, wearing that exact outfit. It's the only school picture where I see glimpses of me that I recognize and like. We had fun. On the way home we ate cheeseburgers and fries and milkshakes at Judd's Pharmacy, sitting at the counter in the back of the store, and we laughed about my temper, our tempers; it was something we shared and attributed to our Italian DNA; and we talked about how I would love the freedom of the public school, how eighth grade would be better.

When I graduated from college my mom drove with me to Los Angeles, where I would start my first job. We drove from Elkhart and we laughed the whole way. We drove up Pikes Peak in Colorado, and by the time we got to the top we found ourselves in a snowstorm and had to drive down a slippery, curvy mountain to continue on. I drove. She sat next to me and nervously ate an entire bag of little after-dinner mints, those mints that my grandmother always had out in a cut glass dish, little refreshing squares of green, yellow, and pink. She kept yelling, "Don't brake! Don't brake! I read somewhere when you go downhill you shouldn't ride the brakes." I calmly said, "Mom, if I don't put my foot on the brake periodically we are going to fly over the side of the mountain and die a cold death." We laughed until our stomachs hurt and tears ran down our cheeks. We got to LA and she unpacked me and I drove her to the airport and we held each other like we would never see each other again. We wept the heavy tears of love and grief, a goodbye that ended up being more permanent than we realized at the time.

My mom will never know Carl. I did not think I could survive saying goodbye to her, but allowing myself to live means accepting that we will never fly down a mountain together again. The more I feel her, the more I feel all of the impossible things the world asks us to bear, the more I think I might make it. I have been walking around for three days, maybe four or even five, since I started writing this section of the book. I can't track time. I lie down and fall asleep. I am alone in a little apartment in Seattle, eating avocados and small chocolate chip shortbread cookies and drinking a lot of coffee and Belgian beer. Today I went to a barber in this city where I am writing. Tyler, originally from New Hampshire, cut my hair and trimmed my beard. He is twenty-three and said "fuck" every other word. "I got your back, man, I fucking got your back," when I told him I'd been holed up for a week and hadn't washed my hair or shaved. I closed my eyes and listened to the straight-edge blade scrape under my chin. I love that sound. It's like sandpaper against wood. I love saying "fuck" every other word back to him.

In a lifetime of very little connection, my mother kept me tethered to something, to those memories of being together and momentarily at ease. I would not be able to access ease again until I met Lynette, and I would not be able to live at ease until I had the courage to say I was and am a man.

I am on an airplane back to Boston, sitting next to a young man with a bad sniffle. He's reading the Bible with a pen and underlining it. I wish I believed in God. I wish I would meet my mother in another time, another universe. She is a good person with a gentle heart. I know she has never forgiven herself for our childhood, for all the screaming and poverty and neglect that came before and after the photo. I know this book will break her heart. I hope she cannot read it, perhaps one gift of dementia for her, for me. She may not know that I am with her when she dies, she may not understand who that man is coming to visit her. I knew when I pushed that first syringe filled with testosterone into my right thigh that I was saying goodbye to my mother once and for all.

CHAPTER SIX

QUEER ENOUGH

SEATTLE, WASHINGTON

There is a delicate form of the empirical which identifies itself so intimately with its object that it thereby becomes theory.
—Johann Wolfgang von Goethe

Alex has been my swim coach for several months now. As Polly, I hated the water, hated to swim, and didn't really know how, but as Carl, I started taking lessons from Alex one year into testosterone, and I love the pool. My body is soaking in all the detailed mechanics of how a body maneuvers through the resistance of water. Alex is a natural coach and he has a way of training me that mirrors my transition, each lesson building on the last. Recently I asked him if he would also do weight training with me. One week we do weights, one week we swim, and some weeks we do both. The nice part about weight training with him is that I'm above water and we get a chance for small talk, which often isn't so small. Yesterday I asked if he might do some training with my nephew, who will be visiting me this summer. That led him to asking about my siblings. I told him about my two brothers, and he said, "Oh your poor mom, she had to deal with three boys." I hesitated for a moment. Should I tell him, "Not really?" But I loved the sound of "three boys." My personal truth existed somewhere in his assumption. I relished the idea of what he was imagining about how my life might have been. I replied, "Yes, my poor mom."

I tell a friend about the exchange. "You aren't out to your trainer as trans?" my friend asks me. "That seems dishonest. He's told you he's gay."

I stumble in my reply. I hadn't thought about it that way. "Are these truths about us equivalent?" I ask her.

"But you think you're queer, too, right?"

I equivocate. "I think the answer is more complicated for me than 'yes' or 'no.'"

"But how can you not be queer?" she says, "Denying your queerness denies the history of activism that allows you to be living this life."

Queer doesn't feel right, but denying it also feels wrong. And Alex is one of a handful of people who have given me a renewed sense of my life in this transition, though he doesn't know it. I want to be honest with him. I certainly don't want to be intentionally dishonest. Our time together is sacred because he is teaching me to know my body as a man, and I don't want to risk disrupting that. I don't think Alex will be transphobic in a harmful way, but I don't want to lose the continuity I feel with him, this present tense sense of myself that I am relishing. Transphobia is so nuanced, insidious, and unexpected—to learn someone was once other can reorient an imagination, and I like how Alex imagines me.

I am being honest when I say I'm not sure what constitutes honesty in this circumstance, because my truths feel multiple and I don't have adequate language to describe that. I am not the first trans man who would willingly default to describing myself as a heterosexual male, yet I have not had a life that has resembled the lives of my two brothers, both heterosexual males. I did not grow up as my mother's son, even if I felt like her son. There is verifiable truth to that in the many pictures of my life as her daughter. But what about what was never visible, what my body knew but no one could see?

You often hear trans people say this, and perhaps Janet Mock was the first trans person to put it in a book: "Not all real women have vaginas and not all real men have penises." But if you replace "women" with "girls" and "men" with "boys," when a baby is born how can we know which girls have penises and which boys have vaginas? We don't. We don't know who is trans at birth because it's not visible. Trans knowing, especially the kind of trans knowing that propels people to change gender markers and decide to live on the other side of the binary they were born into, is a knowing that is shaped over time (sometimes not much time at all) as that knowing rubs up violently against the cultural expectations of the gender you are assigned. A trans man on Twitter once declared, "If only one day a baby could just be born a baby"—if only gender could be allowed to shape itself outside the constraints of the naming that comes with the biology of secondary sex characteristics. But this hope feels dishonest to me. Trans and cis people, and certainly gay people, are invested in the categories of gender and whether to live inside the binary or to stretch that binary in every direction until there is no binary. The entire architecture of our culture is founded on gender—our economy, our rituals, our desires, and our love—even when we queer those rituals or reimagine them, we are still investing in gender and what we think it looks like on the outside.

What is the language, then, to describe a body that has been betrayed by the common biological markers of sex and stretched all the cultural possibilities of an assigned gender and still sees no way through to a livable life? And what about a body that has always possessed an internal knowing that is also sexed and sometimes stereotypical in its gendered desires? How do I describe how my body feels and what might be invisible to you? How am I to be honest with you?

Lynette has a cousin who has two boys. We have watched them grow up on Facebook. The younger is into all things "boy"—football, wrestling, trucks. The older one passionately engages all things "girl." He has dressed as Princess Elsa from the movie *Frozen* for that last three Halloweens. To start first grade, he wanted a lunchbox with ponies on it and his mother persuaded him to get something more gender-neutral. She posted a long meditation on Facebook about what it means to be a good mom (to want to protect her son from bullying), and her disappointment in herself for not letting him be himself. Lynette and I immediately find a lunchbox online that is covered in horses, close enough, and we send it to him. Three days later her cousin posts a video of him doing a pirouette (he also takes ballet), tightly squeezing his new lunchbox. Is he transgender? Is he an effeminate boy? Will he grow up to be a woman, or gay; will he use "they" and "them" and reject male or female pronouns? Whatever unfolds for him, his passion is not for neutrality or a genderless world, his passion is for all the stereotypes of girlhood—unicorns and princesses, ponies and pink ballet slippers. He dreams in versions of gender expression, just not the ones that are usually ascribed to his sex. What is invisible in the body of that little boy princess? What moved him, from the minute he could look for himself in the world, to think a princess was his nearest reflection? This searching isn't gender-neutral, though Disney princesses are definitely a social construct.

There is now an entire body of journalism devoted to exploring what's "wrong" with boys. Why are they more likely to engage in mass killings and inappropriate sexual behavior? As I scroll down the comments section in one of these articles, some parents say we need to be raising humans, not boys or girls, that the problem is gender itself. I think Lynette's cousin is also trying to raise a human who may or may not be a boy, but this doesn't erase sex and gender. He already expresses such a clear sense of himself. My parents weren't pushing me in the direction of masculinity, and no one is pushing princesses on that sweet child. My body knew the places to find its reflection and the reality of reflections is that they come with the baggage of culture, which includes stereotypes like princesses and pink ballet slippers. Toxic masculinity is part of the baggage that comes with my reflection, and I have to contend with how that is a piece of the puzzle. But my toxic masculinity was always a risk for me long before I transitioned, as I ingested masculinity and maleness from my earliest memories and lived out my masculinity in all the bodies I have inhabited.

SEXING THE CHERRY

I tried to sort this all out with my therapist via FaceTime when I started this chapter during a visit to Seattle. This question of my queerness and my honesty is interrupting my sleep and making me stumble through my workouts. Am I too invested in my maleness? Are Alex and I both queers? Does LGBQ have a right to claim the T? Is grouping "nonnormative" (Is that a bad word? Am I not normal?) identities under one rainbow what makes an acronym beautiful? Should I just wrap the rainbow flag around my shoulders and call it a day? After a long conversation with my therapist, I close my computer and get in a Lyft for the Capitol Hill area of Seattle.

Have you been to Capitol Hill in Seattle? There is a rainbow flag painted on the asphalt of every crosswalk! Is this a message from God? Why can't a fifty-one-year-old person who has thought about gender nonstop for his entire life know if he's queer or not? I wrote a dissertation on queer theory! One entire chapter of which is on Jeanette Winterson's novel *Sexing the Cherry*. I spent ten years thinking about the cultural act of sexing a body as if it was a queer cultural act that I thought would account for the fact that I knew then that I was not a woman, that I had not been sexed appropriately. My first tattoo was an homage to the cover of that book, two cherries that sit where my left breast used to be. They barely survived top surgery, and now appear as if they will be eaten by the recently added red-tailed hawk whose beak hovers perilously nearby. Queer was freedom for me then, and in the early stages of inhabiting this new body, it feels more like a box.

When I first met my therapist, unbeknownst to me, I was one month away from changing my name, two months away from starting testosterone, and three months away from stating unequivocally that I am a man. Or do I mean a trans man? Why do I like to say man and leave the trans part off? When I went into her office I described myself as ambiguous—neither male or female—partly because that is how I appeared on the outside and partly because I thought it theoretically accurate. Several months later she told me she almost didn't take me on as a client because she didn't experience me as ambiguous. I ask her to go back to our first few meetings and tell me what she saw:

> *It was more of a feeling and a knowing. I did not see a woman, but I did not see a gender-fluid person either. My clients who identify that way are freed by the ambiguity. Everything about your body language felt hunched and clenched. I felt hunched and clenched inside when I would sit with you. As I got to know you I learned that you had always expressed yourself as gender-fluid, you had found a million ways to convey that, and for you*

that state was lethal and empty. You showed up in my
office the first time in a perfectly tailored man's suit and
ready to die. When you said, after only a few sessions, "I
think I'm a man and that I've always been a boy and a
man," I felt both our shoulders unhunch and our fists
unclench. You relaxed, and I relaxed, and I knew I could
be your therapist.

When I verbally "sexed" myself male to my therapist and
allowed the word "man" to reverberate through my body, it was
the first time I sensed what having a body might feel like. If
this feeling is "honest" or "true," is it biological, cultural, queer,
normative, or a form of a diagnosis like gender dysphoria?

GENDER THEORY 101

The academic project around gender has gone in multiple
directions in the thirty years or so that I've been digesting gender theory. Some theories focus on the differences between
men and women, some focus on the similarities or at least
believe the differences to be cultural and not natural, and
some find the words "male" and "female" relatively useless
containers, ripe to be deconstructed and remade.

It's hard not to feel the very distinct differences between men
and women in a country that now has the permanent imprint

of the #MeToo movement informing our every interaction. The differences as they play themselves out appear politically clearer than ever. Almost every person who has inhabited a woman's body has a #MeToo story, including me. We are a culture traumatized and in pain because of uncontrollable and violent expressions of masculinity—something women have been thinking about and writing about for a long time.

In the late 1980s and early '90s my classmates and I spent a lot of time talking about whether women are born different or made different. In the early days of feminist theory, women focused on biology, shared characteristics of being a woman, like mothering, which were less oppressive and violent than characteristics of being a man. But biology couldn't account for all of the differences between women. Women who didn't want children and women of color and poor women didn't see how they were like the bourgeois white feminist academics writing about women's sameness. Feminists began to focus more on the way what had been naturalized about women's lives was in fact constructed by culture—focusing on things like the wage gap, and the glass ceilings keeping women out of politics and leadership roles, and domestic abuse—differences not located in the sex characteristics of bodies but in the cultural roles women had been assigned.

Feminist theories of difference are now mashed together in the real-time politics of the 2016 Hillary Clinton defeat—

the assertion from many liberal thinkers that any woman's body in a leadership position is preferable to the status quo, period, given the white male faces filling the Oval Office, stacked in cabinet meetings, and marching in the name of white supremacy. It is a politics of body counts, primarily based in biology, but certainly supported by cultural indicators. It is boys and men who are gunning down American's children in their classrooms. Gender difference, an identifiable bodily distinction that, like racial difference is often visible and definable, feels like one road to saving America from all the white men voting in Congress to undo decades of feminist advocacy that made Hillary's run for president even a possibility. And yet, as we hope different bodies with different cultural realities might save us, we know that culture and biology are unreliable. For every Gloria Steinem there can be an Ann Coulter. It is expected that conservative women should vote more progressively around women's issues than their male counterparts, but they often fail to meet expectations. This body problem has always complicated feminism in all of its iterations. As the few women in the White House are now proving, toxic masculinity isn't only a condition of bodies assigned as male at birth. Nothing was more shocking than the statistic that fifty-three percent of white women voted for a president who was recorded bragging about kissing and groping women while his wife was pregnant.

Some versions of feminism also have a complicated relationship to trans identities. In the trans community our feminist nemeses are called TERFs and we spit out the T and the F like we are upchucking some phlegm—Trans-Exclusionary Radical Feminists. These are "women born women" who deny that trans women are women. They believe if you were born with a penis you are invited into privilege and you can never experience the cultural reality of womanhood. Biology comes first, then the cultural experience of biology. For TERFs, synthesis of biology and culture make trans women not women and by extension trans men not men. I saw one vitriolic feminist thread on Facebook talking about trans women competing as women in the Boston Marathon and the unfair advantage they would have over "real" women. These are women who believe in the biology of women's bodies but deny the possibility of the biology of trans bodies. Always, it seems, theories of gender turn against themselves and their premises.

In another example, an episode in the Amazon series *Transparent* contains a scene at a women's music festival where Maura, the trans woman protagonist (played by the actor Jeffrey Tambor) is "clocked" as trans by another woman and is shouted off the festival property as the "real" women scream "Man on the land! Man on the land!" Tears of rage and grief and loneliness stream down Maura's face. For the women shouting, Maura represents the source of their trauma as secondary sex characteristics are inescapable in a woman-born-woman paradigm. For Maura, these women are the source of her trauma.

Queer became the word of the decade in the 1990s because of its inclusive qualities, unfettered by biology. Queer could hold difference and sameness more readily than feminism—including drag and butch and femme and every articulation of the gender spectrum. Men and women could break the binary of gender difference by "performing" the differences that live inside the biology of male and female. Men could express their femininity and women their masculinity and we could all be here and queer and you would have to "get used to it." Queer meant a certain kind of freedom, or as Judith Butler would say, "working the trap you were already in," which implies not that we can simply change clothes and become ourselves, but that the repetition of difference and queerness and the performance of gender could make visible the limitations of the box of biology. We could be "queer as fuck," as we shouted marching down the streets during the gay pride parade, and who was going to stop us—plenty of people, of course, but that wasn't the point. In the frame of queer, talking about homosexuality as naturalized in the body, "I was born this way," was intellectually problematic. Why espouse the idea that homosexuality is part of nature? As the queen of drag performance, RuPaul, would say, "You are born naked and the rest is drag." You didn't have to be born any which way, you could be attracted to whomever you were attracted to and dress how you dress and be who you are.

RuPaul's show *RuPaul's Drag Race* has been on for more than a decade. He is a cultural icon widely credited for bending gender in every direction—famous for saying, "You can call me he. You can call me she. You can call me Regis and Kathie Lee; I don't care! Just as long as you call me." In a 2018 interview in *Vogue,* his queer freedom is written up as an antidote to the egomania of America's current president: "Ego is all about saying 'I'm better than you are,' and drag says 'You are not your clothes, you are not what it says you are on your birth certificate. You are a creation of your own imagination.'"

But even RuPaul's imagination goes only so far. When asked in March of 2018 about having trans women on hormones on *Drag Race*, RuPaul said no. "You can identify as a woman and say you're transitioning, but it changes once you start changing your body . . . it changes the whole concept of what we're doing." In other words, if a male drag performer becomes naturalized as a woman, the performance is no longer a performance. You are no longer imagining yourself, you are embodied in a different way; that isn't drag. The trans community pushed back, and RuPaul doubled down, "You can take performance-enhancing drugs and still be an athlete, just not in the Olympics." After a Twitter uproar, and the threat of losing viewers to the show, RuPaul apologized.

RuPaul has always been the queen of "anything goes." I really had to think about what it meant for him of all people to put a limit on realness and imagination. RuPaul was using the same basis for realness as TERFs, that only "biological men," queer or straight, can do drag. His imagination of drag performance has a limitation when it butts up against real, felt bodies that represent difference, a different sex in this case. As my head spins, I have a long conversation with a friend about this and she puts it in the exact right theoretical terms. She categorizes his response as a form of resentment that trans women on hormones are changing the rules of drag. In theory speak, the signifier can never achieve what is signified. In other words, drag attempts to get to an ideal of the feminine but as drag, what is underneath always belies the capacity to actually be the thing it seeks to perform. RuPaul has made an entire career on coming as close as any "man" can to perfecting the performance of being a woman, but he has not achieved the thing itself, womanhood. A trans woman on hormones, he is arguing, becomes the signified: the performance and the self become one.

In an unexpected twist, he makes my point about my experience of trans identity being, for me, a feeling of embodiment that is not fully explained by the possible ways I tried to imagine myself and perform myself when I inhabited a body without testosterone. I would say, for example, that I cannot perform, that I could have never performed, as a drag king (I speak only for myself here) because I am a man. For me, drag would be to try to perform the hyperfemininity on *RuPaul's Drag Race*.

THEORIES VERSUS FEELINGS
OR IDEAS VERSUS BODIES

When I say, "I am a man," I am not fully able to articulate how "trans" and "queer" fit into the picture in terms of how my body feels and has always felt. I embraced queer in the early 1990s when I "came out" as a lesbian and was writing my dissertation. Naming my desire was the one other time in my life that my body felt electric, different from now, but at twenty-four, I finally understood what "turned on" meant. If having sex with women meant I was a lesbian, and therefore queer, I didn't care, at least initially. The queer box was my only option, but I never settled into it, and sometimes it makes me angry, in the way that anger and grief get conflated in a body, that I had to live as a lesbian to have any kind of life at all. My denial of my queerness is rooted in its own stereotypes, like saying I never wanted to sing show tunes, so I must not be gay. But I only ever looked for myself in the reflection of boys and men. The tropes of masculinity sparked in me an even deeper desire than my need to sleep with women—being visible to the world and seeing myself in a mirror and recognizing me, this has been the drive that has defined me. I do not feel queer in the ways we often think of that word, one that defines people sleeping with someone of the same sex or personally rejecting living inside the gender binary. I sleep with someone of the opposite sex and my gender doesn't feel very fluid.

As I write this, I am notified that I have received an award for my work in the theater. These awards have been created as an alternative to the traditional theater awards specifically to honor women. I worked in the theater in the body of a woman for twenty years, and I know one man is honored each year along with all of the women. I assumed I am being honored as a man. But when I reach out to friends I want to invite to the ceremony, every single one of them says, "How do you feel being honored as a woman?" This hadn't even occurred to me. I write an email to double-check and in it I say, "I would not be comfortable taking an award away from a woman." They confirm I am being honored as a man. But my point is, it is easy to conflate trans men with women, and trans men with lesbian terms like butch, and trans men with people who identify as queer and gender-fluid. The award is conferred upon me for my work as a woman, and what could be queerer than honoring a man for what he accomplished as a woman?

I understand that I am queer and trans culturally. I was announced as a girl at birth and lived her life. Now Alex, my trainer, assumes I was announced as the second of my mother's three sons; I am living that boy's life. This is queer. I am trying to navigate two truths simultaneously—I have never felt queer and I have lived a queer life. The idea that my insistence on my maleness reinforces the very gendered boundaries that excluded me for fifty years doesn't diminish for me the need to inhabit a connection to a self, one expressed in maleness and masculinity. I know I am overcompensating now, wanting to make up for lost time, to be a man. I did queer for so long. I can and will march on the streets for queer rights, for the right of all bodies to sit with relaxed shoulders, palms open, and still, as my feet feel the pavement reverberate off the bottoms of my sneakers, I can relish my masculinity as a truth that gives me the power to stay alive. I recognize this doubling will take more time to feel and understand. I am still on the run from Polly, but her life and experiences are still with me.

Queer was my only option for twenty-five years. My friend who thinks I should come out as trans to my trainer is right, to deny it is to deny the activism that makes my life possible now. And still, I feel so much grief for having missed my boyhood, my male adolescence, my twenties and thirties and forties trying to be a lesbian, never feeling at home in the culture available to me. I wasn't a butch. I loved football and tried to watch it with a group of butches, but I didn't feel like I was with my tribe. Lynette and I spent holidays and parties in spaces that were all queer women. Many of these women are still friends of ours, and that friendship isn't diminished for me by my truth, though for some of them it is. They don't like men and they have a right to distance themselves from my transition. I have a cis, straight, female friend who tells me regularly that I'm the only man she can stand to spend time with. I'm glad for that because I love her, and I hear what she's saying. But I'm at home in the spaces I describe in this book. My happiness, my pleasure, my desire, my work, and my hobbies are connected to my maleness and my masculinity.

Jack Halberstam, a theorist I admire, has been a beacon in the world of queer studies since I started thinking about queerness in theoretical terms twenty-five years ago. In 2017, he published *Trans*: A Quick and Quirky Account of Gender Variability*. I bought the book immediately and turned the pages in search of a better understanding of the transition I was in the middle of. He, like me, is looking for language that can make sense of his life. His project is to bring trans* into language as a gendered term even more inclusive than queer. He describes his attraction to the word trans*—with the emphasis on the asterisk.

The category takes the prefix for transitivity and couples it with the asterisk that indicates a wild card in internet searches; it's a diacritical mark that poses a question to its prefix and stands in for what exceeds the politics of naming and recognition.

I immediately wondered how to pronounce this word, or can it only live in two dimensions on a page for you to know me? Do you have to read about me, or can we meet? The asterisk makes me think of Prince, when he lived as a symbol. I have read so many times in gender theory the need to "exceed naming," another way of saying to move beyond the certainty of identity, to be able to redesign one's house at a moment's notice, to not be determined by definitions that don't fit. My desire for the wholeness that comes with telling my therapist "I'm all guy" is theoretically considered American sentimentalism, the dream of individualism, a body self-contained in its own truth—wholeness is privilege—a privilege I can sometimes access and sometimes cannot. I know wholeness is patriarchy, but for me it also feels like a part of my own becoming, to allow myself this privilege temporarily, in a few discreet places like the gym, so that I can know parts of myself that haven't gotten proper attention for almost a lifetime.

*Trans** is anything but sentimental. Reading the book, I wondered how Halberstam *felt*. He talks about doing top surgery as an architectural project. Had hormonal transition been more of an option when he was younger, he says, he probably would have done it, but not now (he's in his fifties). He describes top surgery as a moving away from the feminine but not toward the masculine. Is that possible? He uses the binary pronoun "he." He gets to name and describe his reality, it's part of why trans* is important to him conceptually, it represents two dimensions in which he wants to live his life. But his description of my understanding of my trans identity felt diminishing, as if I didn't understand my own feelings. For example, when he is talking about the hormones that have allowed me to stay alive, to feel embodied, and to thrive, he refers to them as chemical scripts, scripts that "produce embodiment."

> *The trans* body within such a system names the desire for and the results of a drug cocktail as much as it articulates a deeply felt sense of being in the wrong flesh bag.*

What is a flesh bag, and can a flesh bag have a felt sense? Is my desire to live embodied as a man a desire for a drug cocktail? Does a drug cocktail produce my identity, or does a drug cocktail help connect me to me, neurons and flesh and cells to thoughts and emotions? As I am reading about trans people being fired from their jobs, as I read a suicide note of a seventeen-year-old trans girl, Hope, who even with the support of her family could not transition fast enough to want to live, I can't even utter "flesh bag."

When I began taking testosterone my therapist explained it to me in simple terms that made perfect sense. She describes trans, at least for someone who experiences it as I do, as a health issue. It is not a pathology, but rather like diabetes—the body isn't producing something it desperately needs to live, to feel itself. As my body acclimates to the testosterone, it's like it's coming out of a stupor that I have been in my whole life. Flat words on a page will never convey it to you adequately. I could see more dimension to the world. My body started to want to be out in public. I relished things like traveling and small talk because I could feel others see me and connect to me as me, the man I am. I had been tattooing over my body since I was twenty-four, trying to make the woman disappear. I could sit for hours and let that needle pierce my skin and feel nothing. A year on testosterone and I sit for a tattoo and I cannot bear the pain. I am so sentient now. And for the first time in my life, I feel I am in the world. I am, in certain spaces, a straight white man who loves to spend time with other men—fat men, thin men, tall men, black men, short men, Latino men, gay men, Muslim men, men who drive Lyfts, men who drink bourbon, men who talk football, men who buy sneakers instead of engagement rings, men who lift weights, and men who call me bro. It is to be at home in my house to sit in the barber's chair and have my beard trimmed and talk about Star Wars movies with Stephen, and to talk men's fashion with Travis, and queer movies with Alex. Before I transitioned, these things all felt like home in my head but not in my body. I wasn't allowed the seamlessness of the connection, and to sit with Stephen in his barber chair would have made us both awkward and uncomfortable. Is this a problem with a culture overly invested in a gender binary? Yes, of course it is. But this doesn't change how I feel, and it doesn't change my desire not to disrupt the seamlessness of it all, not to disrupt my training with Alex.

When I started seeing my therapist weeks after my fiftieth birthday, I told her I didn't intend to live until fifty-one. I told her I could not become a middle-aged woman, my boyishness almost gone; womanhood would kill me and I would rather kill myself. No matter how ambiguous I was, the world would keep insisting on "she." When I told her three months later, I had made the decision to take testosterone, she made me promise to give the medication time. She asked me to give her one year, to see how I felt, and then we could talk about suicide again. She was convinced, having been a part of other transitions, that I would feel differently if I had a body I could connect to, that felt like mine. She was right. It defies language and it isn't contained in a diacritical mark.

Back to the question of honesty. Here's what bothers me no matter which way I answer it. If I continue to train with Alex as a man and if I continue to sit in Stephen's barber chair as a man, I reinforce a binary that is detrimental to the comfortably gender-fluid person who wants to feel that same wholeness or the trans man who cannot afford top surgery and hormones but feels no less a man as a result. If I tell Alex and Stephen I'm trans, I relinquish the wholeness I *feel* deep inside my body to be seen as I experience myself—a feeling I never got to have until now. I don't feel queer when I work out with Alex. Am I trying to inhabit a privilege, "all queers be damned," or am I trying to acknowledge a feeling in order to be willing to deal with all that comes with that feeling, good and bad?

A FELT SENSE

Trans people who have chosen to change sexes often describe the desire as "an irresistible longing" or "an irrepressible drive" to live and be seen as the other sex. I see this drive in transmasculine men on social media. Though my guess is many identify as queer, and they are definitely out as trans, they go into funks of deadly depression when misgendered. Why does their queerness, my queerness, need the certainty of language, of specific pronouns, to feel seen?

Lynette and I were out to dinner to celebrate her birthday just a few weeks before I would no longer be misgendered. I had a wispy beard and mustache. A lesbian couple next to us struck up a conversation, "Have you ladies been here before? What do you recommend?" They talked and talked. I sat quietly, frozen at "ladies." "Can we exchange information? We need more lesbian friends!" On the way out of the restaurant we ran into someone I know professionally who called me by my old name, and then as we were walking to our car, bundled in winter gear, a man passed us, saying, "You ladies have fun tonight!" By the time I was behind the steering wheel, I didn't want to keep living, and my wife was pissed that her birthday was ruined by my gender trouble.

What is the language for this felt sense of always knowing the pronoun "she" was wrong? Why, as someone who knew in every part of my overeducated brain that gender is not a binary, that we all contain various levels of masculinity and femininity in both our biology and our expression, could I never acculturate to the feeling of being a woman, a butch, a masculine woman, agender, fluid, nonbinary? I saw an image of a hyperfeminized woman on Twitter exclaim, "I'm fluid as fuck." I believe her. It's not visible in her photo, but I believe what she says she feels. But why could I never say the word lesbian to describe my relationship? Why could I not allow a thread of women's clothing to touch my skin for the last twenty-five years, until I felt old enough to say "No more"? Why could this body not roll with anything the culture had to offer until it rolled into manhood without a stutter or a stumble? What is this experience called? Is a felt sense of knowing spiritual? Or do we not yet understand enough about how bodies and gender and identity work?

I don't have language to describe the 2016 Netflix series *The OA*, created by Brit Marling and Zal Batmanglij, but I intuit some answer to my questions after watching all eight episodes four times now. At its surface, it's a sci-fi tale about a woman who has been abducted by a crazy scientist and she and his other captives create a language between them through choreographed body movements, referred to as the Movements. Marling describes it this way,

> *I think that the Movements come out of something on the other side of technology, that is maybe more ancient and primal, coming from the knowing intelligence of the body rather than that kind of divorced intelligence of the mind.*

In the very first episode, she tells the seventeen-year-old Steve, the embodiment of toxic masculinity, who has just punched a male classmate in the throat, to search for his "invisible you." "You spend a lot of time on your visible self, what about the stuff on the inside?" Steve has the physicality of many a trans man's dream; his perfectly sculptured body appears fully nude in the first few minutes of the show. In an interview I did with the incredible drag performer Taylor Mac, he describes his dazzling stage manifestation this way, "On stage the drag isn't a costume, but something I'm exposing about myself; it's what I look like on the inside." Drag is how he makes his invisible self visible.

I am interested in this idea of an invisible self. I have always said that I walked around invisible for fifty years and that now what could not be seen on the inside is finally alive on the outside. Yes, the outside is a kind of costume but it reflects an inner knowing.

Maggie Nelson takes up both the need for language and its limitations in her book *The Argonauts*, which is partly a memoir about her relationship with her trans husband, Harry. "The answer isn't just to introduce new words . . . and then set out to reify their meaning. . . . One must also become alert to the multitude of possible uses, possible contexts, the wings with which each word can fly." I wonder if the word masculinity can have new wings attached to it in the context of becoming a man after waiting a lifetime. I even wonder if binaries mean something different when culture and biology live out of sync with each other for fifty years and then get synthesized through medicine and a new context. Is a binary inherently bad for someone who enjoys it? Transitioning for me reminds me of being a child on a seesaw, the thrill of weight shifting when your whole body goes from grounded to flying upward. And I wonder about words like "invisible self," "felt sense," "inner knowing"—words that we don't know yet how to make visible, three-dimensional words. Will those words always live flat on a page too? Marling says, "*The OA* is using science fiction to talk about what deeper feelings we have, a metaphor for the poetics that science fiction can spark around you." I think of the hope that Afrofuturism gives to African Americans, something about the expression of identity in a future tense that goes forward and backward at the same time, ancient sensibilities embodied in new stories and new protagonists. My entire purpose in telling you my story is to find words and metaphors and images that can make the invisible visible, but more importantly, can make my invisible known to you in its feeling, a feeling that is not reflected in trans* or queer and is not visible through the body parts I was born with.

While I'm still exploring some of these concepts, I visited the college classroom of a friend and shared some of my early writing with students. A woman who identifies herself as a lesbian is appalled by what I like about my masculinity. "I know a lot of men, and they aren't like you. You like all the things I hate about masculinity." I ask her, "You mean gyms and bourbon and barbers?" She expresses confusion about her own declaration, "I mean, I guess, well, I guess you're right, I don't know." I understand her emotional response. It's a gut response to masculinity, a gut response to be offended that I take pleasure in masculinity and attempt to box it in a binary, a response that has been earned by men all over the world. I hope she rereads what I've written and I hope I've written it better now. I hope masculinity can gain new wings, because it's a word I like and one I recognize is in a state of serious crisis.

CHAPTER SEVEN

WHITE MASCULINITY

BOSTON TO ELKHART

> It was important for him to believe that he'd spent his
> life among people who kept missing the point.
> —Don DeLillo, *White Noise*

My wife and I are on our way to my parents' house. We drive Interstate 90, which is a direct line from our home in Boston to theirs—Massachusetts, New York, Pennsylvania, Ohio, Indiana. One highway, eight hundred and eighty miles. It's April 2018, and this is our first cross-country drive since my transition, our first time together en route to my small-town Midwestern roots. Lynette and I, as we continue to heal our marriage, are learning to travel as a white, heterosexual couple. I'm outfitted like I'm in my mid-twenties, the decade of my life I most mourn missing as a man—I'm bearded, wearing overpriced sweats, exclusive sneakers that "dropped" at 3:00 A.M. and all the guys like me (but younger) woke up to compete to buy before they sold out, and I am always, always, in a Chicago Cubs baseball hat. My integration into the straight white America of middle-aged, middle-class couples who road trip across the northern border of the US, instead of paying the money to fly, is seamless. Every time we stop, some white man starts up a conversation with me. Lynette is in disbelief. "You're such a guy's guy," she says. "I just don't get it."

It's true. I fit right in with all the white dudes along this interstate. The guys who really love to chat it up with me are usually about my age, maybe a few years older, but they think I'm a younger guy, and they find me irresistible. We meet John Bolton and his wife in a Hampton Inn in Ashtabula, Ohio—it's not really John Bolton, the conservative politician and US national security advisor, but he looks just like him: bushy white hair and what they call a walrus mustache. The *New York Times* wrote an entire op-ed about the significance of Bolton's facial hair:

> *Mr. Bolton's disregard for shaving norms is a faithful reflection of his fierce independence, and his general disdain for established political ground rules and diplomatic norms. . . . He is the ego in conflict with the superego of the political establishment: Negotiations and treaties are for wimps, and so are razors.*

Mr. Bolton of the Hampton Inn has a similar disregard for shaving norms, as well as fashion norms, his '80s-style relaxed-fit jeans, golf shirt, and white Reeboks (these are back in fashion, called "dad sneakers," and selling for over a thousand dollars, but he doesn't know this) make him indistinguishable from all the other fifty-something white guys we have seen pulling off the Interstate. He sees me get out of the car with a bottle of small batch bourbon. He and his wife are grabbing pillows and sleeping bags from their Hyundai as if they are on a camping trip. They have done this drive before.

"Hey," he says, smiling, "don't be partying it up too loud tonight; we gotta pull outta here early tomorrow. You a Cubs a fan?"

"Yeah," I reply. "Since birth. Grew up in Indiana and we don't have our own baseball team."

"No kidding, we're from Noblesville, about forty-five minutes out of Indy, you know it?"

"You bet I do. They had a pretty good basketball team when I was in high school. I'm from Elkhart."

The conversation continues the next morning at breakfast. We're all heading out early. Lynette and I learn Mr. Bolton and his wife have been on four cruises, all to the Caribbean. "Cruises are the only way to vacation, you have to try one." The local Fox News affiliate is blaring in the room with the free breakfast buffet. Suddenly all of our eyes catch the story of the two black men arrested for sitting at a Starbucks for two minutes without ordering while they waited for a friend. It was just two minutes! We all look at the screen; there are two other white couples eating waffles and boxed eggs, and everyone around us quickly looks away. Mrs. Bolton starts to choke on her bagel. Mr. Bolton stands behind her and says, "You need me to hit you in the back?" He looks at me, "I like to have an excuse to hit her." He thinks he's funny. I suggest some water and he runs to get it. There is a lot of joking about how she doesn't know how to swallow at her advanced age, and we wave and head our separate ways.

I have never been visible like this before, and Lynette and I have never been welcomed as a couple into the fold of Middle America. We can be in Ashtabula, Ohio, and not worry about whether I might get killed for looking a lot like a man but not. Our life as a straight white couple is more astounding the more we move around the country together. Being a white man married to a white woman is just so pleasant, so easy, and so terrifying. What have I gotten us into?

When we arrive in Elkhart and land on Bristol Street, we are greeted by a Confederate flag waving high atop a pole in front of one of the 1960s suburban-style homes that pepper my parents' once-wealthy suburb. My parents bought theirs after all the rich people left and the homes had been on the market for years. MAGA signs are in full bloom as we turn into my parent's driveway. My father is ill. His kidneys aren't working and he's just come out of surgery. My parents are on the verge of collapse. My mother's dementia is making it impossible for her to track that my father is seriously ill. His mind, by contrast, is as sharp as ever, but his body is wrecked from years of abuse—alcoholism into his thirties, chain-smoking until a quintuple bypass at age sixty-five, Type 2 diabetes since his mid-fifties, never a lick of exercise. None of us thought he would ever make it to seventy-seven. But here we are. My brothers and I are realizing our worst nightmare, having to take care of a man whom none of us have ever liked, who never gave a thought to anyone but himself—a scared, mostly mean man who has taken advantage of all of us, and now expects us to come running to his bedside.

BECOMING OUR FATHER

Our entire lives my father, whenever he was home, has been sitting in a blue leather recliner barking orders at us. It's like a sitcom on toxic white masculinity, *All in the Family*, but over time the politics sound more liberal as my father moved from staunch Republican to a more moderate Democrat. The channel buttons on the television remote control are erased by the wear of his thumb switching the channels from westerns to sports to news. It's total control, all of us held hostage to his cruel sense of humor and his tightfisted attention that centers only on himself. Whenever my brothers visit with their children, he won't change his viewing patterns. Kids wanting to watch cartoons are simply out of luck. If any of us, brothers and mother, leave the television room our name is instantly called, summoned back to watch a replay, or to get him an orange juice, or a fresh cup of coffee, or a bowl of sugar-free ice cream, or just to listen to whatever he is rambling on about because he never stops talking, never stops narrating every damn thing he thinks or does or plans to do.

My father was an OSI agent (Office of Special Investigations) in the Air Force and his job was to sucker homosexuals into outing themselves, getting them kicked out of the military. He was a smooth talker, and he bragged he could get anyone to break down in their own shame. He tells the story of how he would take a man out to a bar, get him drunk and talking, and pretty soon he could see the guy was going to confess that he was gay. My dad admitted to feeling bad, to almost wanting to stop the conversation before the reveal. "These were nice guys," he tells me. And he reveled in his ability to manipulate other men. This is how a little guy can have power. He was a salesman of one sort or another his entire life. He went to college at Indiana University, where he delivered pizzas and waited tables to pay his way. In his senior year, he missed his Spanish final when he overslept after a night drinking, and he wouldn't have graduated, but he told his professor that his mother had passed away, so he was allowed to take the test late. My grandmother really died about sixty years later. After passing the exams to be admitted into the FBI and receiving his rejection in 1966 in a letter from J. Edgar Hoover (the gay man who was five feet, seven inches exactly), because he didn't meet the height requirement of five feet, seven inches, he became a used-car salesman. He would boast that he could convince anyone to buy anything, making a rust bucket Pinto seem like a shiny new Cadillac with the power of his persuasion.

My father is hyperintelligent; he can answer all the questions on *Jeopardy!* His chatty personality was always a big hit at work, at least to start, but he could never put his brains and popularity together into a successful life. No matter how much money he made, he was always broke. No matter how far up the ranks he rose in a job, something would happen and it would all fall apart. He was making great money managing recreational vehicle stores. Elkhart is the RV capital of the world. But one day he used the company credit card to gamble and was fired by his boss, a woman. I learned how men talk about powerful women when he came home that day, unemployed.

During his Republican phase, my father helped me become a racist and a homophobe. My single greatest shame, that I have never told anyone except my wife, is that in 1984, at the age of eighteen I cast my very first vote for president of the United States for Ronald Reagan. My second biggest shame, or maybe equally shameful to that vote, is that in junior high I would call my older brother, Tim, a faggot when we would fight. I didn't know what that word meant. I had never knowingly met a gay person. But I learned quickly how to be as cruel as my father. Tim was a quiet and sensitive guy who sat in his room and drew and painted all day and night, rarely dated, and had few friends, and I knew how to take him down with one word. When I came home from graduate school and told my father I was gay, he didn't speak to me for a year. And my racism, where to start? I think of my racism as something that is in my feet, part of my foundation.

My father's racism, if one can write about gradations of racism, is less overt than most white people I know in Elkhart, but that isn't anything to brag about. I ingested a lot of my racism from him. Indiana is basketball country, and the biggest bond I have with my father is sports. The rare moments he was home when I was a kid, we would watch our favorite teams, the Indiana Hoosiers and Notre Dame Fighting Irish. He would yell at the black players from his recliner. He would call them wimps. Every time a black player would fall to the ground holding an ankle, he would shout at the television, "Get a hook and just drag him off the court." He was a Republican for many years, primarily because he thought the taxes going to black welfare moms were robbing him of his income. Ronald Reagan was his hero then—an actor and a conservative, a dream come true for a movie-obsessed white trash kid from Centralia, Illinois, who had served in the military. I can't blame my biases all on my dad. Italians hated black people almost as much as they hated themselves because they were considered dark-skinned too, and part of being Italian was separating your skin from an African American's skin. My mom's Italian family certainly augmented my father's lessons.

One day I am sitting outside my therapist's office. I am living as a man and I am working on a theater piece about liberal white racism and I am in conversation about the effects of racism every single day. Like a lot of open-minded white men, I think I have confronted my racism rigorously. I have easily separated myself from all the white men who have criticized the play, oozing white supremacy in attempts to deny it. The door to my therapist's office opens and an elderly black woman with a cane hobbles out as I walk in. I don't realize what I'm thinking until two days later. But what ran through my head, almost unbeknownst to me, was, that's cool, my therapist must do pro bono work. Obviously, my unconscious mind thinks all elderly black women are poor and can't pay for their own therapy. My Reagan roots reveal themselves.

Please, I beg my therapist, purge my father and Elkhart and American history from my body.

My brothers and I do shifts coming to Elkhart, in our birth order. My older brother arrives in time for the surgery and leaves the day after, I show up right after the surgery and stay a few days, and then my younger brother comes to do his stint. We are on a group text centered on three things: status updates on my father's health, plans to sort out the financial mess that is my parents' lives, and fearful musings on how much we are like him. Or how we're not like him. We share confessions and worries and insights.

CHRISTIAN: The thing I'm noticing the most is that Dad makes everything about Dad . . . but I do see how much like Dad I am.

ME: If you've ever thought about anyone other than yourself, even one time, you're not Dad.

TIM: It would be easier if he weren't so appreciative of our help—he has that car salesman thing—every once in a while, he thinks for a moment he can say the right things to keep you engaged.

CHRISTIAN: He narrates everything he does. Announcing what he's going to do next. Gonna check my blood now. Gonna weigh myself now. Gonna see if I can poop now. Jesus, man . . . just do it. And now that I think of it, I think I do that.

TIM: Dad is such an asshole to Mom. I've had to put him in his place like four times already today. It's the main reason I don't want to leave the two of them alone. He's just toxic.

As my brothers' texts come, I imagine my father's obituary with the headline "He was just toxic!" How many men have died who should have been buried under this headline? I don't want to be a terrible son, a terrible person, but I have been fighting my entire life to unravel my white masculinity from his. He is not the worst man in the world. He had a flare for violence, a raging temper, and the ability to unleash it with a belt on my behind, but he could never kill anyone. My father bought a gun when I was in college. He was growing this greasy little tail of hair down the back of his neck and sporting a thin mustache and carrying a handgun in the glove compartment of his car. He looked like some sleazebag right out of a spaghetti western when he flashed the pistol at me while I was home one weekend. The next time I came home, the gun was gone. "I was afraid I might accidentally shoot myself, so I sold it."

As my wife and I pull into my parents' driveway, all I can think about is how to be a man in this impossible situation, how to overcome my training, how not to resemble my father.

A few months before we drive to Elkhart, I have a dream. I am floating in space, high above the earth, looking down. I see a cardboard cutout of my father below me, a two-dimensional likeness dressed in an orange jumpsuit. The cutout is calling me, pulling me down as it is spinning into a black hole, into a swirling, sucking vortex right out of a Star Trek movie. Toxic white masculinity and my father are black holes, with a magnetic energy field. As I live more comfortably as a white man, I better understand the gravitational pull toward all I have learned from him.

How do I, how do we, explain toxicity? Is everything a white man does toxic in some context? I think of white men I know expounding on the virtue of empathy and the power of art to transform a culture and then holding secret meetings with other men to destroy the careers of the women who threaten them. They are good in one context and they are toxic in another. At another time in my life I might have called this behavior hypocritical. But now I see it as a kind of doubling that white men do, the way they convey an outer and inner self. They know the right words to say, and perhaps some parts of their bodies believe these words. But as they say one thing, they do another, performing the predictable behaviors of patriarchy and misogyny. They hold on to not knowing something about themselves that others witness. How do white men begin to see the parallel nature of what they say they believe and how they behave?

My father does not double for me during his illness. I can see only one thing and I am trying to distance myself from him to escape what Polly knows in order to create Carl. We are in his home. He has had a stent put in each kidney and he has a catheter. He has cancer. I am in the TV room with him. We have just had a brief argument about the black men arrested in Starbucks. He thinks the woman had the right to call the police. He is in the blue leather lounger and is watching *Tales of Wells Fargo*, a western TV series that ran from 1957 until 1962. He watches it every single day at 5:30 P.M. The catheter is leaking through his diaper. "I'm miserable, I'm so miserable. I can't do this." I lift him out of the lounger with one arm, get him to his feet. I hold the catheter. He is only peeing blood now. I get him into the bathroom. In 1996, after five years of graduate school, I started volunteering in a housing facility for people at the end stages of AIDS. I know how to do this. I put on latex gloves, release the lever on the catheter, and drain the blood into a measuring cup and record the cc's. I put a towel underneath him, and I pull down his soaked pajamas, and pull one swollen foot and leg out at a time. I pull down the diaper, and blood and urine drip out all over the towel. His scrotum looks like a pink helium balloon. It is not recognizable as any form of power, just a useless leaking organ. I get a washcloth and soak it in warm water. First I wash his face, gently moving the cloth over his forehead and cheeks and eyelids, then underneath his neck and his arms. I rinse the cloth and I wipe his penis and in between his thighs and down his legs. He doesn't have his partial teeth in and he is drooling all over the top of my shaved head, the drool running down the left side of my forehead. He hums the entire time, except when he says, "Now that you're my son, it's okay for you to do this."

A GOOD WHITE MAN?

I carry three photos in my wallet that give me comfort. One is Lynette in eighth grade wearing cat glasses, her natural beauty peeking out from underneath her "geek" phase. Another is Lynette airbrushed and heavily made up for a glamour photo shoot she did in 1998; her black leather bustier makes me horny. The third is of Frank D'Amico, Lynette's father, on a Navy boat during the Korean War, dressed in a white T-shirt, his skinny arms and chest wrapped in another private's arms, two buddies at sea. My relationship with Frank gave me a glimpse into what it might feel like to be a son.

In 2009, right after Lynette's mother passed, we moved from Minneapolis to Chicago—two hours from my parents' home in Elkhart and several hours from Frank and his home in St. Louis. Frank was our first visitor. He came too soon. Our furniture hadn't arrived. There was nowhere to sit, a guest mattress on the floor, and food had to be ordered in, which violated our Italian hospitality values. The windows in our old bungalow had been painted shut and I hadn't had time to pry them open. The air in the house was thick and "foggy," as Lynette would complain. I was preoccupied with starting a new job and was feeling impatient and agitated, but Frank insisted on coming. He took us to an old Italian supper club on the Northwest Side in Irving Park and leaned into the table midway through the dinner to say, "I had to see for myself that you were both okay, that you moved out of happiness and not grief." And then he paid the bill. Frank came several more times to see the theater I was making. He didn't especially like live theater or going out in the evening, but he loved me. He loved Lynette even more.

Frank was solid ground under my feet. He wasn't powerful or persuasive or ambitious or frightening or certain like most of the men in my life. He was curious, quiet, and attentive. When Lynette was on her own and broke, a few years after she moved to Minnesota, Frank bought her a Ford Escort. She insisted on a station wagon. He kept saying, "What does a young, beautiful woman want with a wagon?" He set up a payment plan for her to pay him back, and every check she sent him, he put in a savings account. He never said what he was doing, just sent her a check for the entire amount when the car was paid off. When Lynette and I had to sell our house in Chicago for another job move, Frank knew we had taken a hit in the financial crisis. I wouldn't tell him how much we lost on the Chicago bungalow, but one day a check for eight thousand dollars came in the mail, just the right amount to make us whole. Frank moved slow and steady and with purpose.

When I was in college, my father called me in my dorm room and my brother in his and told us to meet him at the bank right away. Our college tuition was late and he didn't have the money to pay it. We hadn't received any warning, but rather found ourselves at the bank signing a credit card contract and each of us taking a cash advance of several thousand dollars to pay our tuition bills. The credit cards had to be in our names because my father's credit was maxed out and he didn't have the money to pay his own bills. I remember being awash in fear that I would get kicked out of college for delinquent payments. My body knew what the threat of creditors felt like. Our phone would ring several times a day when I was a kid. My mom wouldn't answer because most of the time it was either the mortgage company threatening to foreclose on the house or the electric company threatening to turn off the lights. I learned to live in fear of the ring tone, of my mom crying and pleading for more time whenever she did answer. I was happy to sign on the dotted line if it meant I could stay in school and avoid the embarrassment of having to leave college because of debt.

My father, with the echo of my mother's voice in the background, still tells the story of the sacrifice he made to pay for our college years, as if he would have been able to retire with a condo in Florida and a small fishing shack, his purported dream scenario, if only we hadn't permanently broken him financially. He took out a credit card in my brother Christian's name when Christian was in his late twenties, with a fifteen-thousand-dollar limit. He advanced himself ten thousand of that in cash and then called Christian and said, "Hey buddy, I got you a credit card. It's got five thousand left on it, don't go crazy but I thought it might help you out." He made borrowing ten thousand dollars from my brother, ten thousand my brother never had, sound like a good deed. One thing about my father's sleight of hand: we never knew what hit us.

I didn't really know how to describe a good man until I met Frank. And I never knew what a father did until he became mine. Frank wasn't anything like the other men I knew. Born in 1927, he was nothing like his own brothers. One brother was a furniture salesman who aspired to be a writer. He wrote a book that he tried to convince Lynette to edit and publish by stuffing six thousand dollars into her purse after we visited one Thanksgiving. The book was titled *Women Are Bitches*, and six thousand wasn't enough. The youngest brother was a devout racist—I couldn't be in his house after President Obama was elected. And then there was the oldest brother, whom I never heard say two words, because he wouldn't speak to a masculine-looking woman.

Frank chattered in circles of uncertainty until Lynette would finally yell, "I have no idea what you're talking about, stop rambling!" He never made more than forty thousand dollars a year. In his second career as an investment broker, his advice to Lynette and me in early 2008 was to buy Ford Motor Company stock. Frank wasn't handy. He couldn't fix anything. He wasn't athletic, he never exercised, and he never watched sports. He woke up and put on a suit and tie and went to work every morning until he was eighty. He was beloved by his coworkers. He was thrifty. His purpose in life was to leave money for Lynette and her two brothers, and he denied himself to save for his kids.

Frank and I first met in 1998, he a Republican and myself a Democrat, and we constantly argued politics. A fiscal conservative, he was anxious about his money and taxes, and had voted for George W. Bush in 2000. Frank couldn't wait for Lynette and me to visit. He liked to get me revved up about a proposed tax cut or some union negotiation. I always came armed with statistics on the disproportionate ratio of defense spending to social programs. We had deep ideological differences, and we took pleasure in our time together trying to convince the other to be more moderate. I think on an occasion or two we might have even influenced the other's thinking. Frank's politics were never about people or groups of people. The only people I ever heard him speak ill of were the white fundamentalist Christians at Lynette's brother's church. Lynette's mom, Ida, by contrast, was preoccupied with "the blacks" moving into her once all-white suburban neighborhood and lowering the property values. I am sure Frank harbored racist perceptions and beliefs and some homophobia, and he had conventional notions about women, but he took people on their own terms, and he made judgments based on experience, not preconceptions.

Lynette's mom called me "the landlady" for the first several years Lynette and I were together. She didn't want to accept that Lynette would not have a wedding and children with a man. Frank and I were sparring partners and friends. He naturally treated me like a son, a reliable one whom he trusted to care for his daughter. "She has a PhD," he told everyone, as if that made me an expert on everything. He was an older white man who thought I knew more than he did on some subjects and whom he turned to for advice. We talked about finances and cars and his time as a radio operator on a transport ship in the Navy. He asked a lot of questions about the theater I was making. We talked about clothes and shoes, and I begged him to give up his yellowing white Rockports. "You're good-looking, Frank. No reason to dress like an old man." I helped him mow his oversize lawn. When we met up with him in Buffalo, where his brothers lived, he always insisted I drive. We watched Turner Classic Movies together—we both loved old Fred Astaire and Ginger Rogers dance numbers. He knew I was Lynette's husband.

There wasn't harmony between Lynette and her brothers and me. Her brother James is a monosyllabic Italian man obsessed with his physical fitness. In her brother Mark's case, his Italian dominance turned into a 1950s white fundamentalist Christianity, where women do the dishes and have babies and fawn over him, and men are men and women who are women don't include a queer, feminist sister. It was Frank's final wish when he became ill that Mark and James be good to Lynette. "Italian men look out for the women in their family. It's their duty," he told them. Frank's death was peaceful and seamless. We worked together to make him comfortable. As he was taking his final breaths, Mark asked us to pray and played his favorite church song. We held hands, praying Frank was with Ida in heaven:

Jesus has overcome
And the grave is overwhelmed
The victory is won
He is risen from the dead

We shared memories of Frank attending his nieces' volleyball games, reading stories to his great grandson, shouting directions at me to make my pizzelles not so thick. We would never be together like this as a family again. Lynette and I would never listen to a song about Jesus again. I would never believe in heaven again. But nothing was easier than giving Frank what he wanted in those final moments.

FOX NEWS

In the last few years of his life, Frank was a man divided in two. He started watching Fox News on a loop and saying things I didn't know how to engage. He was watching segments that referred to Barack and Michelle Obama's fist bump as a "terrorist fist jab," or Bill O'Reilly telling the son of a 9/11 victim to "shut up," and the famous claim by Megyn Kelly to kids that "Santa is just white." It seemed as if overnight he was sounding crazy like a fox, one day defending waterboarding the prisoners at Guantanamo: "What if one of you had been in those towers?" Or talking some insanity about the "War on Christmas." He and his brother Vinnie would sit in front of the TV in Buffalo, where Frank spent a lot of time after Lynette's mom died. Vinnie would say over and over that someone should kill that "n___ in the White House" as Frank stood by quietly. Our debates turned to shouting matches, mostly me yelling because Frank never yelled. This was a man who had over more than a decade taught me about goodness. Frank had come to our gay wedding and wept with joy. When he was in a rehab facility in St. Charles, Missouri, after breaking his hip, he beamed at the nurses, telling them "This is my daughter and her wife, they just got married." His next line might be "Obama isn't an American citizen," and that line would sit right next to Lynette asking, "Where's your winter coat, Dad?"

"I gave it to one of the nurses at the hospital [where he volunteered every week] for her son. I can get another one."

We are all contradictions. We are all doubling as ourselves. Lynette and I are doubling as queer and straight now. Mark, the most devoted family man I know, doesn't object to immigrant children being torn from their parents' arms at the border. I love my father in some abstract way, and I can't be near him. I miss my mother terribly, but she has been gone from me for almost two decades now, and I am not with her as she withers from Alzheimer's. What defines goodness in a world where we are all split in two, trying to preserve a self and create it?

Frank became increasingly anxious and doom-saying. He believed, because Fox News told him it was true, that we were near end times, and he worried that Lynette and I wouldn't get to see our old age. My father is increasingly anxious as he faces his own end times. All he can think about is the next doctor's appointment, the rash on his back, the oxygen level on his tank, the money my mom spent at the grocery store to buy the expensive ice cream she likes. As America doubles as a democracy and an oligarchy, it's hard not to believe we are approaching the end of something, the power of white masculinity, misogyny, and patriarchy either pushing us toward civil war or breathing its last gasp.

CHAPTER EIGHT

LOCK HIM UP

ELKHART, INDIANA

The state of creation is this dream state where suddenly,
obeying an unknown need, you burn the house down,
you push a friend off the top of the mountain.
—Hélène Cixous, *Three Steps on the Ladder of Writing*

I meet my mother at the emergency room entrance of
Elkhart General Hospital, and we walk down a mile
of corridors to elevator D and the cardiac unit, where my
father has been admitted for an irregular heartbeat on top
of his cancer, failing kidneys, and breathing problems. The
hospital is located on the border of McNaughton Park, where
I played softball and endless games of tennis and rode my
bike along the Elkhart River—my best memories of a city I
have tried to leave behind. There's a dispute over the name
of the city, but the land was purchased in 1831 by a wealthy
doctor named Havilah Beardsley, from a half-French, half-

Potawatomi chief named Pierre Moran. So it's likely named after a Native American chief, Mihsheweteha, meaning elk heart. I was a straight-A student, but I never learned anything about the land where I played. The Pierre Moran Mall never meant anything to me but the stores inside. The erasure of Elkhart's history is in the Beardsley landmarks and the park named after John McNaughton, an early and successful capitalist. Elkhart, like America, built its foundation on the lies it tells itself about its origins.

My mom is getting sicker. My father's decline is unraveling all of her routines—routines that are a lifeline for someone with dementia. We are walking through the hallways of the hospital where she did an internship twenty years ago while getting her social work degree. A lot of people know her here, and she keeps introducing me, this bearded man, as her daughter, Polly. The looks on people's faces suggest they think she's gone crazy. I consider twirling my finger around my ear to confirm their suspicions. As we get to my father's hospital room, we come upon a conversation he is having with the nurse about his insulin.

My father is an expert on everything and he is giving the nurse a lesson on diabetes. In his world, women don't know anything, but male doctors are infallible. The nurse is in training and she is in way over her head. They are in a shouting match:

"I am going to tell you one more time, I have been managing my insulin perfectly for twenty-five years!"

"I understand that, and it's not that I don't believe you, but we have legal protocols that I am bound by law to follow."

"Your protocol is wrong!"

The conflicting protocols are shouted back and forth for what feels like twenty minutes until I see myself get out of the chair I had parked myself in and shout at him, "You shut the fuck up! Don't you say one more word." I have scared the child nurse, but he shuts up. I call his endocrinologist, set up a meeting with the nurse's supervisor, and put a plan in place to manage his diabetes better.

I'd arrived in a frenzy. My father had texted me that morning that he was being admitted to the hospital, that things seemed dire, and I knew my mother couldn't be alone, so I bought a ticket at 9:00 A.M. and was on a plane by noon and in Elkhart by five—the good son who would do what needed to be done, knowing full well the chaos my father created in living would be replicated (and then some) in dying.

Before learning the full picture of his condition, my dad begins to plan his departure from this earth. Visitors start to come because he has let everyone know that "everything is shutting down," and he's planning on going into hospice. He doesn't know what that means. He talks about it like he will be euthanized. "They will give me some morphine and I will just go to sleep." I keep texting my two brothers that I have no idea how sick he is because Dad sick and Dad well are pretty much identical, except for the twenty pounds of water weight he is carrying. But after five days in the hospital with him, I start to believe he isn't going to make it. He is nothing if not convincing.

His bridge partner of ten years arrives and brings him a pamphlet on holistic approaches to treating cancer. Has he met my dad—Jimmy Dean sausage's biggest buyer? The bridge partner asks me how my kids are doing. He thinks I'm my brother Christian. I tell him my daughter is becoming an accomplished hair stylist and colorist, which my niece is. Two more bridge players come up and ask to pray over Dad. I start to imagine a Christian rock group named the Fundamentalist Bridge Players. Then his most foul-mouthed friend, who he has played golf with for years, stops by. He's been born again since his wife died a year ago. He tells my dad, "We have to get you right with God," and forces us all to hold hands and pray over my dad around his hospital bed. Another friend comes and brings him Ensure. My dad has said a thousand times that he can't eat, but he is knocking down those Ensures. This guy asks me, "Is your sister Polly coming?" "We are coming in shifts," I say.

Transitioning for a time is like pushing Polly off the top of a mountain. I have to burn down the house of Polly so that Carl can come out. It is an origin story, a state of creation, an unearthing of the him who has spent his whole life locked up, shape-shifting, sticking his head out periodically, but mostly living in a fight-or-flight state, just trying to survive. Polly was my friend and protector, but I wasn't her and she wasn't me.

The stories of him, of the ways he came to assert himself, are stories of going crazy. He was my madman in the attic, confined like the women in nineteenth-century gothic novels; he was looking for a storyline to set him free. Carl was Polly's mental illness. She locked herself up to keep him safe.

The first time he went crazy was at a girls' slumber party at Sandy Biondo's house in the third grade. It was his inaugural overnight in a crowded sea of Barbie sleeping bags. Giggling and baking cupcakes, doing each other's makeup in the bathroom upstairs, and staying up until 3:00 A.M. As she lay in his plain, light blue sleeping bag, his heart began to race uncontrollably. She felt the racing pulse in her neck, something she would do a thousand more times in her fifty years of crippling anxiety. She had never felt his heart beat so hard. His stomach began to churn and she ran into the bathroom to vomit. Her first panic attack and his first attempt to escape. Her last slumber party.

The second time he unraveled enough to make her sick was her junior year of high school. She had been chosen to attend

P. CARL

Girls State in Indianapolis, a week of mock government and civic leadership run by the American Legion Auxiliary, where girls from around Indiana live together in a college dorm, run for office, and design political policies. She was a huge hit and so popular that she was nominated as one of three girls to be interviewed to represent Indiana at Girls Nation in Washington, DC. Jane Pauley, media personality, was a Girls Nation notable alumna, as was Ann Richards, the former governor of Texas. When a group of girls ran into the dorm bathroom to surprise her with the news, he disappeared into a bathroom stall, crouched on a toilet, hiding and sweating from head to toe. He blew the interview on purpose—telling the judges he didn't give a shit about Girls Nation, let one of the other girls go. She went back to Elkhart and he got in bed for an entire summer. She lost fifteen pounds and her parents and relatives told her she looked great.

By the time they both were thirty years old, death seemed inevitable. They spent their thirties together in a psych ward, protecting him, keeping him alive inside her. Mental illness is when knowing tackles not-knowing to the ground. Sometimes you need medication to not know things for stretches of time so you can keep getting out of bed. She medicated herself into not knowing him. She bought them both time.

Entering a psych ward is to be in a dream state, to believe that if you are locked up, confined to a sterile room with no mirrors, forced to wear pants with no belt and shoes with no shoestrings, you will be safe. I was diagnosed as bipolar at age thirty and my first hospitalization came soon after. I was trying to finish my PhD, wandering aimlessly through theories of identity, and writing about the failures of academic feminism when I spiraled into a severe depression and became too anxious to drive, ride my bike to the library, or even leave the house. I saw a psychiatrist who prescribed me lithium. Weeks later, not feeling any relief, I sat out in my garage with a sharp piece of glass, trying to slit my wrists. I took myself to the emergency room and was admitted to the psychiatric unit. I was prescribed more lithium and an antipsychotic medication, Zyprexa. In the months that followed I gained sixty pounds from the Zyprexa, and bipolar would be a misdiagnosis that I would carry around for twenty years—a misdiagnosis that at least recognized I was living between two poles, between two selves. In a culture overrun with diagnoses and medications to treat them, there are a lot of us practiced at not knowing. The sane among us get locked up and the white male politicians are allowed to roam free and spread their insanity like germ warfare.

One day in a group therapy session in what is probably visit number ten to the psych ward, I am sitting next to a middle-aged Midwestern blonde from Shakopee, Minnesota. She is unremarkable; from the outside she looks less unkempt than some, a veneer of solidity that makes me wonder what she's doing here. Then she tells her story. Her thirty-year-old daughter, her best friend as she described her, had planned a big fiftieth birthday party for her. She had set up catering, had had a cake delivered to her mom's house. A few hours before the party, she had been with her mom setting up tables and making a playlist, and then left to go to her apartment to change clothes. She said to her mother what she said every time they parted, "I love loving you," and walked out the door. She never showed up for the party. She had gone home and hanged herself. This mother, that veneer I had misrecognized, was a husk, all that was left of a body destroyed by the unknown becoming known. "What had I missed?" she asked. What was lurking inside the body of her daughter that day? What was underneath the party planning and the love of loving her mother? What could that young woman not bear to know, not bear to feel?

My psychiatrist, Dr. Evelyn Nesbit, age seventy-one, dressed in her usual leopard-print shirt and short black leather skirt, with her wild, blond-dyed hair, pulls me aside during one stay in the psych ward. "You have great potential," she says. "With any luck and hard work you can still lead a full life." She gives me a pep talk, shares a little of her personal struggle with bipolar illness and convinces me to take monthly injections so I am always medicated, don't have to remember to take pills, and can stabilize. A nurse comes to my room later in the day and injects Prolixin into my thigh IM—intramuscularly. Within a few days there is no inner and outer me, there is no knowing and not knowing. I am a ball of twitching muscles, sitting at a coffee shop, reading the same sentence of a book over and over and trying to keep my eyes open. This dream lasts a month. I think I will never wake up. The only thing I will ever inject into my thigh IM again is testosterone.

At its worst, the purpose of a psych ward is to normalize you back into a community that is anything but. Its purpose is not to heal you, but to make you stay sick so that you can function alongside the lies of a country steeped in them, so you can function alongside the lies you are forced to tell about yourself. We are all doubling in order to live, and the psych ward tells you to squash that inner knowing. It's simply not useful if you hope to thrive. At its best, psychiatric care gives you tools to let your inner knowing walk alongside the insanity of the world and create survival tools to trust what you know and survive the gaslighting and discrimination that seeks to burn down your house.

The truth of our beginnings can be hard to stomach. My origin story reveals itself to me in the course of my dad's illness. It's the story of an inner feeling, a kind of knowing steeped in my trans body and my traumatic childhood. The two come together in my dad's hospital room. I am a man now, his son. He talks to me like one. His swollen penis is something he insists I look at constantly, to gauge if the swelling is up or down. He says, "P, P, P—I got a story for you. You can't tell anyone this, but when this thing first started to swell, I was like, but does it work? While your mom was at work, I went into the bathroom and I masturbated." He can't stop smiling and laughing as he tells me this. He hasn't had a moment where he hasn't complained about his misery until now.

"And you know what, it worked. It still worked. It made me feel like a man."

My father telling me stories of how he jacks off instantly makes me feel bad for what my brothers must have endured over the years. I sit in that hospital room for six straight days and I listen to him talk about himself. He is sicker by the minute, and I think I can tolerate anything now, knowing that his misery and my misery are near an endpoint. He says things like "I only have two regrets, just two regrets. I wish I hadn't drank and I wish I hadn't smoked. If I hadn't smoked, I wouldn't be here right now. I would have lived a lot longer."

It's hard not to suggest he might have other regrets, like

gambling away all his money so he and Mom have nothing now, not even enough money to bury themselves. Or perhaps he regrets not having relationships with his children and grandchildren? That's one I thought of right away. As I'm pondering all the regrets he should have, he gives me clear instructions on what he wants to happen when he dies. He shows me a short playlist on his phone with his favorite songs, which includes Mario Lanza and "Memory" from *Cats*.

"I want to be cremated, and then I want a celebration of life, a Saturday afternoon celebration of life so people can travel who want to come."

He never asks about my mother. Her decline is soul-crushing. He never asks how any of his visitors or children are doing. He writes his own obituary at least ten times, instructing me each time to get out a piece of paper so I don't miss anything. I act like I'm taking notes on my iPhone. He gives me a list of his assets:

Gold Notre Dame pendant with two diamonds—worth a few hundred
Green jade ring—probably worth the most of anything he has, get it appraised
Gold and black Bulova watch—not worth much but people always comment on it
A stamp collection

A coin collection
Baseball cards
An antique Mother Hubbard cookie jar—worth about
   five hundred

"Divide it up however you want."

———

This hospital room is throwing me back into the psych ward of my thirties, the smell of bleach, the endless manic chatter, the pink food trays, waiting for the expert in a white coat to take the pain away. I am caught between Polly, that little girl who is now the one residing deep inside, and Carl, the man who emerged to take her place at the surface. My craziness has reversed, my knowing and not-knowing switching sides. My fear began with my father, this man, and all I can think as I sit here is *please don't talk*. "The state of creation is a dream state." I have to push Polly off a cliff or Carl will never have a beginning. How can Carl live comfortably as a man knowing what Polly knows? I wish, as I sit in my father's hospital room, to be in the psych ward, to not know this man; I long to be medicated.

———

Overnight my father goes from planning the celebration of his life to suddenly feeling significantly better and making a game plan with the doctor to beat the cancer. The minute I realize he's going to live a while longer, I fly back to Boston and my brothers come to relieve me. My father's texts start immediately. It's like I'm still in the room with him, listening to his endless self-absorbed chatter as I'm walking to the train:

DAD: A much better night. Might be making me stronger to die.

DAD: Pills, pills, pills!!!!

ME: So glad you had a better night. That's great!

DAD: Better today. Just walked the entire hallway at my request.

ME: Wow, that's amazing.

DAD: But still in the woods, P.

ME: I will be curious to hear what the doctor says tomorrow.

DAD: Hoping for rehab. But not if I can't see the results.

DAD: Ordered two eggs, bacon, and toast. We'll see.

DAD: Ate it all.

ME: I'm really glad you're feeling better. You are going to need to think really quickly about how to help Mom. She cannot be alone, so you have to think about who will take care of her and how she will be set up.

DAD: I don't have any idea.

DAD: Need decisions on myself to decide more.

ME: A man's number-one responsibility is not himself, but how he cares for his wife. This is the most important thing, and she may in fact be sicker than you. You will need to call her doctor now that you're feeling better. She needs whatever strength you have.

DAD: Not able to deal with her doctor at this time.

DAD: I don't need to be told about a husband's responsibility.

It was that last text that reverberated through my whole body and landed in the pit of my stomach. I was walking to the train and had this sick feeling that Polly could never be killed off, that Carl was saddled with this origin story, his masculinity permanently tainted by her knowing. One night when I was about nine or ten, we waited for Dad to come home from work so we could get a Christmas tree. We ate dinner. No Dad. We stared out the window waiting for his baby-blue Cadillac Escalade to pull into the alley. 7:00 P.M. 8:00 P.M. 9:00 P.M. The Christmas tree lot was closed. We watched some TV, our favorite Christmas villain Mr. Heat Miser in *The Year Without a Santa Claus,* and went to bed. The next morning, he showed up around seven to take what he called a bird bath. He would be out drinking and playing cards and then he would come home, splash some water on his face and under his armpits, change clothes, and go to work. You had to admit the guy had stamina. I said something like "Dad, where were you last night?" I was always the only one with the guts to say anything, and I had a way of intoning these questions with a sneering disappointment that enraged my father. "It's none of your damn business what I do." I knew to run. I knew calling him out put my whole family at risk. My brothers would always say, "Polly, why did you have to say something, can't you just keep your mouth shut?"

When I get my father's text, "I don't need to be told about a husband's responsibility," my body flinches. I run the rest of the way to the train, remembering the time my father didn't pick me up from my bank teller job and I had to walk four miles home. When I asked "Where were you?" he dragged me from the chair I was sitting on and slammed me against the wall, bruising my shoulder. "It's none of your damn business where I was." The faster my heart pounds, the more I feel the complexity of what I know now. I was always the son willing to risk everything to tell my father the truth, and I was always his daughter who had no business challenging his manhood. I am a trans man who still lives in fear of my father's rage, even as he lies helpless in a hospital bed. My origin story is trans and trauma, it is both Polly and Carl. I text Lynette what my dad texted me and she replies, "Lock him up in a nursing home."

CHAPTER NINE

POLLY

**ELKHART, MINNEAPOLIS,
TOKYO, CHICAGO, BOSTON**

Devastation. That's what makes people migrate, build
things.

—Tony Kushner, *Angels in America*

My body knows intimately the life of a girl and a woman. I am struggling with how to tell you about the things that happened to me because of my gender. I watched Anita Hill testify and now Christine Blasey Ford. Is there some kind of perfect tone a woman must use? I cannot ever forget Brett Kavanaugh crying out his victimization, yelling of conspiracies, trying to turn the tables as abusers do, his red, twisted, enraged face captured in dozens of photos, a face etched in the psyche of every woman who knows what's true. When I try to write the stories of being a woman, I sound defensive. If we once thought depression lived in the spleen, where is my defensiveness located and could I use a linguistic scalpel to remove it? I write this chapter several times until the stories become disemboweled. My greatest anxiety in my transition is to lose track of what happened to Polly, to do to a woman what was done to me. In some ways, I know this has already happened, because Polly could spew toxic masculinity, and Carl tries to prove his maleness sometimes with a less-than-enlightened bravado. Mostly, though, I lived the life of a woman at the mercy of patriarchy and misogyny. I cannot forget. I can't run from Polly—what kind of man would I be then?

My first day of graduate school in the fall of 1991, I am twenty-five years old and I am in the administrative offices of my new department. I am introduced to another first-year graduate student. He suggests we go for coffee. He tells me about his life in Nigeria and lets me know right away that his uncle is Chinua Achebe. I have read *Things Fall Apart*, an early exposure for me to the idea of precolonialism, and I love talking about books; the conversation is free-flowing and engaging. As my coffee grows cold because I don't even drink coffee yet, and as the banter winds down, I ask if he's taken the bus. I'm fretting over public transportation, having never used it before. He invites me to his place for tea so he can show me how to navigate the city.

We take a bus to his apartment. We walk up two flights of stairs. He puts on the tea and walks over to the apartment door, locking it from the inside as he pockets the key. My strongest memory is of the ominous feeling that shook my body watching the key slide into his pocket. The things a woman never forgets, like laughter, or the black leather belt he was wearing that day. He takes off his shirt and begins to take off his pants. I tell him I have to go. "No, no, no," he tells me. "We will get to know each other." I begin to shout, "Unlock the door, let me out!" over and over. I am pulling at the door frantically as he walks toward me. I am no match for his thick, six-foot frame. A few seconds feel like an hour. I know I am about to be raped. He unlocks the door, I run down the stairs and the three miles home. The phone is ringing when I get to my apartment. How did he get my number? "I think you are beautiful, please come back." I hang up. The calls go on for weeks. I am afraid to go to campus. I never tell anyone. I know, because every woman knows, that if I show up on the first day of school and accuse a man of, of what? What do I call what he did? I wasn't physically harmed. I know reporting what happened will jeopardize my entire graduate career, and classes haven't even started yet.

Several months later I learn that he is harassing under-graduates; one in particular is afraid for her life. I tell my department chair, "I am coming forward now because I want to confirm that what these women are saying is true." He wonders why I didn't report this when it happened. I know why the next day when I walk into the shared graduate student office. None of the women of color and few of the men in my department are speaking to me. I am the white woman who accused a black man of sexual misconduct; the politics are problematic. The men who run things will matriculate Achebe's nephew in a matter of months. Though when I start to do the research, I find that he's not Achebe's nephew, but rather the nephew of Christopher Okigbo, a famous Nigerian poet but not one that I would have known at the time. He did collaborate with Achebe after this incident, so I can imagine he knew him, and he also knew the name to drop to get my attention. I learned from another graduate student who learned from one of the faculty that he had come from the University of Iowa with a reputation for harassing women and Iowa wanted him out. In a sleight of hand very familiar to me that I don't know the details of, he was quickly handed his PhD from the men running my department and then he disappeared. Problem solved. Nineteen years later, my thesis advisor emails me a news story out of Reading, Pennsylvania. After many years teaching undergraduates at Kutztown University, he met up with his wife at his sister's home, sat across the table from her, shot her several times in the head and chest, then shot himself in the head. He was sixty-four and she was thirty-seven. I imagine the trail of women with #MeToo stories attached to him. I feel partly responsible for the death of his wife.

I went to college with a sweet, gentle woman who lived down the hall from me in our all-girls dorm. A Midwesterner from Ohio with a welcoming smile and kind eyes. My roommates once rearranged our dorm room while I was at the library and decided I didn't need a desk. Sue and her roommates were my respite. I stayed with her in France once when we were in college, and she became a beloved high school teacher who taught French and took her students abroad to experience the culture as she had. After filing for divorce and a restraining order, her husband murdered her with a shotgun in his car in front of their home, the three children watching from the window, then he killed himself. Sue's son says they were watching with the hopes that their parents were going to reconcile. He ushered the two daughters away from the window and called his grandparents, Sue's parents.

Like any woman alive, I can keep going. The stories of threats and violence and terror are part of every woman's life and the lives of her circle of friends. The stories aren't always connected to horror; more often they are about the ways men undermine a woman's knowing and the aspirations that come with it.

I am in Tokyo early in my tenure as the artistic director at the Playwrights' Center in Minneapolis when I receive a call from my communications director to tell me "we have an emergency." The press needs to speak with me right away. "Can't it wait?" I ask. "I'm in the middle of a rehearsal here." "It can't wait," he tells me. A playwright and former board chair of the Playwrights' Center has written a letter about me and sent it to the press and the charitable foundations that give us money. My mind is racing to try to think about what I could have done. Did I clumsily fend off a sexual overture and inadvertently piss someone off? Is there a staff member who reached a limit working weekends and I missed it? Did I give offending feedback on somebody's play? He tells me via a bad phone connection, "The letter complains you've focused too much on taking the organization national and left local playwrights behind." I feel a huge wash of relief come over me. There is some truth to this, at least the part that I have focused on growth and increased fundraising opportunities. "This can wait," I say. But a woman with ambition needs immediate intervention.

I've come back early from Tokyo and am at a conference room table in the basement of an 1880s church that houses this sacred space for playwrights in the Seward neighborhood of Minneapolis. I am interrogated by reporters and foundation officers about the letter, a scandal. I am sitting on my outrage hoping this will pass, but news stories are published and extra board meetings are scheduled and six months later a foundation president tells me she may not renew a grant, that she's still sifting through what happened. I hang up the phone and throw my keys across the office. I storm out of the building, get in my green Honda Civic, and start driving. I don't know where I'm going. I pull over to the side of the road next to a lush green park a mile or so away from my office where kids are playing soccer, and I call Lynette, choking and gasping in tears. She is at work and calls a friend who comes like AAA roadside service to rescue me. I end up in the psych ward, suicidal. I have never had an outburst at the office before, the keys thrown against my own office wall, not thrown at anyone. The harm I plan is toward myself. I must be crazy. My brain can't make logic out of a situation, my detached body goes unhinged. A man's conviction never has to be logical or legal or true when it becomes destructive and unstoppable and makes a woman doubt her sanity.

My sister-in-law says something that at the time I take with great offense. "It's like Polly gets in a skirmish with some men at work and then lands in the psych ward. I don't think she's bipolar, just too sensitive." In hindsight, she wasn't far from the truth. When I look back at all those hospitalizations in my thirties, they came as I tried to assert my power, my intelligence, my leadership ability as a queer, white woman. After each slap down, I thought I must be insane, a rage and frustration turned inward, a sense that I was a constant fuck-up, not worthy of living. My father had taught me early on what my big mouth would cost me, and every man who came after me in those years of trying to make my mark on my profession replayed those childhood traumas in my body, causing a physical and mental collapse that I believed was, as the doctors told me, the flip side of mania, the depression that comes after the grandiosity of thinking your ambition matters. But who was really crazy? If we learned nothing else from watching the Kavanaugh hearings, we learned that women asserting their truth and their power and their PhDs make some men crazy and red-faced—men who will go to any lengths to put down, threaten, and erase the threat of a woman's reality that impinges on *their* ambition.

And let's pause for a minute. If you're a man, like me but not me, you might wonder what parts of the stories I am telling are forgetting, as Blasey Ford was accused of, what really happened? It has to be more complex than "I was just doing a good job and that made some men angry." How many times have I read about sexual harassment and wondered what parts of the story I didn't know, or doubted that a woman was telling the truth? What is she leaving out? I distinctly remember siding with Bill Clinton during the Monica Lewinsky scandal because she said she wasn't a victim. I didn't want to believe women were so vulnerable, so disempowered. At the time, I also didn't imagine the trail of women Clinton might have abused. As a woman, I would have rather been bipolar, something I could take medication for, than been treated like a woman—something I could not control.

A colleague and I attend a meeting together to develop a project with a local queer youth group. He says to me after the meeting, "This is going to be perfect for you. You'll have a lot of fun with this one." I begin working on a new play with the group and attend rehearsals in the evening twice a week as planned. I send an email update about the project and my colleague replies, "We need to discuss this. I am concerned that you are too focused on queer issues." When we talk, he is adamant that I am off mission with my own "personal projects." My brain cannot make logic out of this either. The collaboration and my participation in the project had been his idea.

I am in the sixth grade. My father is never home and he watches TV or sleeps when he is. He is not warm or affectionate. We are in the basement, our television room. There is no carpeting, just a cold cement floor with a worn rug thrown over it and a rattan set of two chairs and a couch that my mother found at a yard sale. The television is in a big, boxy brown cabinet, luxurious for the early 1970s; the TV is our most prized possession, and the Cubs are playing baseball on the WGN Channel 9 broadcast out of Chicago, one of three stations we watch. He is home in the afternoon. Is it a weekend? I am not sure, but I remember the sun coming through the basement well window, creating a glare on the television. I am surprised to see him. "Do you want a massage?" he asks me. "Huh?" He might as well be asking if I would like him to buy me a BMW to put into the garage until I turn sixteen. "Okay, sure, I guess." "Get on all fours," he says. "You're becoming a woman. Your breasts are beginning to show. I like watching you change." While I am on my hands and knees, he pulls my T-shirt over my head, and leaves it covering my face, a strange smothering, my small breasts dangling, while he gets down on the rug and crawls over the top of my back and begins rocking himself on top of me. It's a quick "massage," and I feel uncomfortable and confused. I stand up and put my shirt back on and I never think of that moment again, until I ask a therapist about it at age thirty. Whatever that moment was, it never left my body, proof that I was a daughter once.

There was the white male porn addict who everyone in the office knew about, who more than one woman had walked in on while he was glued to his computer screen. My white male friend complained to me daily about him, but did nothing. I went to human resources and filed a written complaint on behalf of the women who reported this to me, bound by the rules of the institution to do so. An invincible white man, the porn addict's best friend, took me to dinner four months after I filed the complaint. "I know what you did and I wanted to fire you, but human resources wouldn't let me!" The vice president of human resources showed him the letter without telling me. He was stunned by my betrayal, and the chill that had grown between us now made sense. I learned I wasn't the first person to turn in his friend, and this wasn't the first institution that had protected them both.

In the process of transitioning, of becoming the very thing that had made my life and my career a series of threats and clashes and near firings, I started hearing everything at high volume, like the repetitive droning while being trapped in an MRI scanner—all the language used to talk about women piercing my tender new male body. Men talk about women in ways that I must have been numb to before my transition. In a heated conversation about creating programs to make the theater more gender-inclusive, a white male colleague gets frustrated with me. "I don't get your concern for women and gender as a social justice issue; plenty of women attend the theater." I wasn't talking about the older white women who buy tickets, but the women artists and queer artists and queer audiences who have been made nearly invisible in the stories we see onstage. He implied later in the conversation that my gender and queer preoccupations were racist.

One day, fully grounded in my male body, I listened to two men talk about a female CEO. "What's with her hair, and those clothes? She has no gravitas. It's hard to look at her when I'm talking to her." Another man at lunch with me referred to a woman who had failed to respond to an email as a heifer. I start to feel the misogyny of everyday conversation on behalf of Polly and what she endured. I also began to think about my own complicity in conversations like this, the ways in which women join these conversations with men at the expense of other women. My body feels the shame of it for the first time.

Meanwhile I am being heartily welcomed at restaurants and hotels and by the parking valet and the guy at the men's clothing store and the Lyft driver and . . . I suddenly feel all that I had been denied, all that women are still being denied. I don't have enough imagination to know what women of color feel. Becoming a white man showed me how as a woman fighting for equality I had only been rearranging the deck chairs on the *Titanic*. The injustices I had experienced as a queer, white woman come at me with the same intensity that I can now feel Lynette's love and anger, or the newly coveted beard on my face.

*You cry, but you endanger nothing in yourself. It's like
the idea of crying when you do it. Or the idea of love.*
—Prior to Louis in *Angels in America*

I turn to Tony Kushner's *Angels in America*—a text I have taught numerous times. Kushner is a prophet in the ways he exposes human vulnerability and the fragility of white masculinity. I am looking for a way through. How do white men in positions of power endanger something in ourselves? Can we learn from that brilliant moment in the play when Louis is talking to Belize about race and says, "What? I mean, I really don't want to, like, speak from some position of privilege and—" The sentence ends there. Kushner knows not to finish it, because that is where Louis speaks from in this exchange. He thinks his theories of race are equivalent to what Belize knows through his lived experience. I have heard so many white men use that same opening qualifier. One way not to speak from privilege is not to speak at all. There are others ways too, but this can be a good place to start, to simply not finish your sentence.

I am having a trauma response right now. I can't catch my breath. I wrote "not to speak" and then I felt Senator Lindsey Graham in my body. What is the purpose of this chapter when a man like that can mow down women as a way to never endanger the lobbying money he will get when he leaves the

Senate? After the riveting and truthful testimony of Christine Blasey Ford against Brett Kavanaugh, he rages at the injustice done to a white man, "This is going to destroy the ability of good people to come forward because of this crap." He wants to personally ensure we never come forward again. He and his ilk will never stop speaking.

> You can't live in the world without an idea of the world, but it's living that makes the ideas. You can't wait for a theory, but you have to have a theory.
> —Louis, *Angels in America*

I don't believe anymore that it's a new theory of inclusion or economic policy that will save us. We have enough data to know that it's bodies that are tripping us up. All the men referenced in this chapter who are still alive know the theories, hold well-considered, if in some cases despicable, political positions. They would all identify themselves as "good men." In *Angels in America*, Prior says, "Louis, he can't handle bodies." Louis doesn't want to be around the lesions, the secretions, the suffering that comes with AIDS. Men of every political viewpoint cannot handle bodies, the ones across from them nor their own. Women's bodies elicit a rage that no theory seems to be able to undo. Men sit around a table and they are brutal with one another. They yell, they pound fists, they make cutting jokes about one another, and often they hash things out with a modicum of success. When they leave the conference table, they shake hands and grab a drink together. They can handle one another's bodies. A woman who pounds her fists never gets a second chance. Her body is limited by the gestures it can make and the words she can say and the volume at which she can say them.

My body has never conformed; it's from this vantage point that I understand how privilege can't be fully known when sitting inside it.

> God splits the skin with a jagged thumbnail. . . . He pulls and pulls till all your innards are yanked out. . . . Then he stuffs them back dirty, tangled, and torn. It's up to you to do the stitching.
> —Mormon mother in the diorama, *Angels in America*

I wish I had written these lines to describe what a gender transition feels like, at least one at age fifty. Transitioning and trying to leave womanhood behind split open my skin in an entirely different way than living as a woman did. When trying to escape Polly, she refused to be let go of like the strong woman she was. I'm finding the entirety of my entrails of my insides and trying to stuff them back in this body. Perhaps we must all yank out our own innards and stitch ourselves back together, to transition together and acknowledge all the ways that we are forced to double.

Kushner wrote *Angels in America* to give us hope, to believe as we all want to, all of us who fight for social justice, that "the world only spins forward." This is Kushner's most important theory in the play, and it's what keeps us all fighting for cures for AIDS, and the right to marry whom we choose, and the right to live in the gender that is ours. I keep thinking of the grief and anger I felt watching the play twenty-five years ago as a newly out queer woman volunteering in a hospice facility for men dying of AIDS; and the grief and anger I feel now, twenty-five years later, watching the revival of the play on Broadway as a white man realizing the world didn't spin like I thought it would. I write as Kushner did in his introduction to the play, "on the edge of terror and hope" for the women in this country.

CHAPTER TEN

TRAVELING WITH MEN

ITALY

Italy claimed no defensive reasons for fighting. It was
an open aggressor, intervening for territory and status.
The Italians were more divided over the war than any
other people. . . . Not surprisingly, it was a conviction
that made no sense to the great majority. This is the
story of that conviction: who held it and who paid for it.
—Mark Thompson, *The White War*

There are people who would make war . . . there are
people who would not make war. But the first ones
make them do it.
—Ernest Hemingway, *A Farewell to Arms*

In June 2018, I was in Italy. The previous year, my best friend
of almost thirty years, Lee, and I had planned a trip to the
Dolomites in northern Italy, near the Austrian border. We were
going to celebrate his fiftieth birthday and my first birthday on
testosterone. Lee and I had met in graduate school. We both

went by another name and gender then. We were roommates, political activists, and fellow travelers, and now we were two trans guys and two men in the world. We have become ourselves in both overlapping and parallel lives. In graduate school we came out to each other as lesbians on the same day. Lee's first lesbian lover was a woman named Polly. I had never known another Polly, but there was another graduate student at the University of Minnesota with my same first name, and Lee had fallen for her. There are parts of a friendship you can't make up. He and I were feminist activists. We joined a group called the Lesbian Avengers in the early 1990s and splattered paint bombs over anti-abortion billboards. Lee was a serious anarchist and I was his wannabe sidekick. His motto was "A theft a day keeps capitalism at bay." We shoplifted books and food to survive the financial predicament of graduate student finances and as a form of devout political action.

Lee has organized his life around his passion for social justice, but his natural habitat is the outdoors. Our need to be connected to our bodies is the unbreakable bond between us. He transitioned eleven years before I did, he is a year younger than I, but he has mentored me through this transition, taking each step as the truth it feels like to me, until another truth arrives. He's the only person I trust who gets it from the inside out. We have mountain-biked in Moab; hiked in Canyonlands and Glacier National Park; we visited all the ruins in the

Yucatán Peninsula; snorkeled in the Caribbean; biked from Brooklyn to the Rockaways and swam in the Atlantic Ocean; biked through Maine; our genders morphing with the photos that accompany each trip. I admire Lee. He's always in better physical shape than I am and I crave the way our friendship pushes me past my own points of comfort and endurance. If I weren't so competitive and he weren't so adventurous I would have missed some of the best experiences of my life. This is our first time traveling together as two men. Last year's trip was canceled because my knee collapsed. It feels like a hundred years ago—four months on crutches, before I went home to see my parents in Elkhart after a year on testosterone, when I was only beginning to live as a man, only beginning to know what a body feels like. Since then, I have been training six days a week—swimming, lifting, rowing, individual therapy, couples therapy—I'm in the best shape of my life and I think I might even be able to keep pace with Lee.

Lee has been thinking about trekking the Dolomites for years. He has climbed Mount Kilimanjaro, hiked the Pyrenees, all trips I didn't think I could physically manage. The Dolomites have been on his top five lists of summits for years. Though Italian, I would have never thought of going myself, daunted by the physical requirements of trekking through a part of the world with a reputation for creating some of the worst conditions for war in the history of battle.

The Italians waged war against Austria-Hungary in World War I from 1915–1918 in the Dolomites not because they were at risk of being attacked, but because they aspired, despite a weak army and economic position, to be more powerful than they were—no matter how many lives needed to be sacrificed for a few more feet of land. In the end, they gained very little but lost over a million men with another million wounded over the three-year course of the war. Today, I ascended Mount Lagazuoi along the Austrian front. The topography was more formidable than I could have anticipated. The rock is soft, a combination of limestone and dolomite; it's soluble and it's easy to lose your footing. In these mountains, harsh weather patterns move in quickly. One day we found ourselves frantically trying to get off of a mountain as dime-size hail pelted us and lightning and thunder reverberated. There seem to be no flat stretches in this vertical expanse of three hundred and fifty thousand acres. On several occasions the Italian troops charging the entrenched Austrians caused the Austrians to stop shooting and implore the Italians to turn back; the Italians were too easy a target.

As I hike, I can't stop thinking about my grandfather, my mother's father. There is a photo of him in his army uniform, saluting, the middle finger of his left hand missing, lost to a bullet. The family lore is that he fought on the Italian side, but he came to the United States by himself in 1913 at age nineteen and became a citizen in 1919. This information is on his US passport application from 1923, when he requested to take a short vacation to visit his parents back in Italy. When I ask my mother about it, when her Alzheimer's is progressing rapidly, she says in a rare moment of crystal-clear lucidity, "He fought with the Americans as a way to become a US citizen. He was sent to France and was shot in the hip and finger and was classified as a disabled veteran. That's how I went to college and graduate school for free." But I only learn this after my trip, so during the entire hike I am imagining myself walking side by side with my grandfather a hundred years ago. My Italian relatives clung to the story of an Italian soldier fighting on Italian soil with his people. I did too. I am the same height as he was, five feet, three inches—both of us little men, not ideal for marching and climbing. Today I am climbing to almost ten thousand feet. I started with a ninety-minute ascent, then a thirty-minute descent almost straight down to a vivid blue-green lake, then a two-plus hour uphill on switchbacks to the peak. Lee hiked a little farther than me in order to swim in the lake, but I knew I needed all my strength to get to the summit. I am passing old bunkers and tunnels as I go. WWI is famous for trench warfare, when fighting shifted to being more about defense than offense. The Italians, with military leadership that relentlessly clung to the offensive charge as its primary strategy, were completely unprepared. I understand why now. This is not land that allows you to move quickly enough to go on the attack—the conditions defy a soldier's most aggressive training. How did my grandfather or any man survive here?

After several days of this up, down, up, down, up, up, up, up, up, up, up, down, down, down, down, down, I am beginning to feel the weight of my pack on my knees. All of my conditioning couldn't prepare me for the pounding my legs are taking. Walter, our guide, says there's no training program in the gym that can prepare you for this. I am carrying about twenty pounds of weight: two liters of water, some snacks, a rain jacket and rain pants, a warm fleece, and a change of underwear. I cut the top off my deodorant tube and leave the book I am reading behind to keep the pack as light as possible. Soldiers carried closer to sixty pounds, and significantly more by 1916, because of extra ammo and steel helmets. One night at the hut where we were staying, our hostess was talking on the phone when lighting struck the receiver and knocked her to the ground. A tough mountain woman in a dirndl when we arrived, she looked pale and shaken the next day. I wouldn't want to be wearing a steel helmet in these mountains. There's still snow in places even though it's July, and on one hike I slip on ice while attached to a cable during a particularly difficult descent. I struggle to pull myself back up because there's no traction. While ascending one summit we meet another guide. As we stand at the mountain's edge, a young climber walks up to join our conversation. Not clipped into his harness, his foot slips, and he catches himself a second before he falls a thousand meters. We are not at war and staying upright and alive is a challenge. I can't imagine life in a bunker here, though emotional bunkers are everywhere as I try to reach summit after summit.

I am sitting in a hut below a glacier; the water for the hut comes from glacier melt. We can't shower here because water is at a premium and as the snow melts and turns pink from drifting Sahara sands, the water will run out very soon. The borders, though firmly etched on the map, are porous. There is a doubling reflected in the people and the history. Everything is Italian *and* German. World War I is present tense. A population born and raised in Italy identify as German. "German is our first language, Italian our second," a woman tells us as we ride a gondola to the foot of Sassongher Mountain. She is from an Italian city near Tyrol. Tyrol has gone back and forth between Italy and Austria, and the people who live on the Italian side identify with their Austrian roots. There is an older man in one of the huts dressed in a World War I Austrian uniform, down to the round steel-rimmed sunglasses. Does he know Austria lost the war? The exchanges between travelers move easily between Italian and German and English. The food and the accommodations are culturally bipolar—pasta with ragu sauce followed by a warm apple strudel or a wiener schnitzel with a tiramisu chaser. We drink locally made schnapps or indulge in a shot of grappa.

As I'm eating a typical Italian breakfast of coffee and croissants accompanied by some cold bologna stacked on a plate and being served by the hutkeeper in the dirndl, I am aware of the German family who has been assigned to the table next to our group. We have been in proximity for about a day now—a husband, wife, teenage daughter, and younger daughter, perhaps seven or eight years old. The father and the older daughter have an easy rapport. I look over and he is tending to a blister on her foot, asking where it hurts and gently applying one of those special blister Band-Aids to her heel. He helps her with her gear and throws a rain poncho over her head and backpack—"Perfect," he says, and they go off to hike in the rain as the mother and younger daughter wait for the weather to improve. The tenderness of this gray-haired father in spandex hiking pants putting a Band-Aid over his daughter's blister jolts me back in time. I am mesmerized by their ritual of preparing for the hike—their ease with each other, their obvious connection and familiarity. I try to think about a single moment when my father tended to me this way. I can't come up with anything. Did he ever apply a Band-Aid to me or to one of my brothers? Once I cut my thumb on a food processor blade. I was thirteen and home alone, it was a warm summer day, during the brief period when my mom worked at my uncle's shoe store. I went to the neighbors and they called my father at work because my mom was alone at the store. "You don't need stitches," he said from his desk on the other side of town, but somehow the neighbors convinced him and he finally picked me up and took me to the emergency room at Elkhart General. After checking me in, he left me in the waiting room to get coffee. I was sitting next to a rough-and-tumble biker guy who said, "Let me see that . . . that's nothing, I could sew it up for you." He showed me all the scars on his arms and hands he had stitched himself. While the doctor was suturing my thumb, the nurse kept asking, "Where is your dad?" The doctor giving me instructions: "You will need to wear this bandage for ten days, then see your regular doctor to have the stitches removed. Don't get it wet, cover it when you shower." I was trying to remember everything, and looking toward the door. When the doctor was finished, the nurse handed me my instructions, "Be sure and give these to your father." I walked into the waiting room and saw my brother Tim. He had just gotten his driver's license and a yellow VW bug, and my dad hadn't wanted to wait.

Lee doesn't like the idea of being tethered to a guide and to someone else's schedule, and going with Walter means going with three other people—all Americans. Our group includes a couple from Portland and a single woman from Houston. I know our traveling companions will not be able to keep up with Lee, and I am certain, because I know him so well, that he will be irritated by that, but the Dolomites are serious mountain-climbing, particularly because of the dangerous and rapidly changing weather patterns. I had convinced Lee a guide was a good idea.

This trip and our little cohort inadvertently become a course in gender studies. Bill and his wife, Heidi, are in their mid-fifties and have been together thirty years with one child. Erica has just turned forty and recently ended her relationship with a male partner of ten years. Bill talks endlessly from our first breakfast together about all he has achieved in outdoor adventure: hiking, skiing, cycling, spelunking, etc., etc., etc., etc. I remember Hemingway's description of the decorated soldier Ettore in *A Farewell to Arms*: "a legitimate hero who bored everyone he met." Heidi says, "I walk five miles a day, but I've told Bill this is above my pay grade." Erica has over-packed and Walter starts pulling stuff out of her bag and tossing it to the side, "No, not this, not this, not this." Her quiet, high-pitched voice, a few extra pounds around the midsection, and brand-new hiking boots make me assume, wrongly it turns out, that she will never keep up.

Overconfident American cis men never disappoint. Bill is the worst hiker in the group. He's fit enough, but unsteady on his feet, dangerous to hike behind as he trips and stumbles on the soft rocky paths, and his fear of heights instantly reveals itself by the way he clings to the stone walls of the mountain at every overlook. In one of my favorite moments of fragile masculinity in history, as we are in a steep ascent, he yells out ahead, "Walter, Walter, can you stop? Do you have any anti-bacterial ointment and a Band-Aid? I burned myself boiling an egg this morning and I have a blister." The look on Walter's face is one for the ages. "Anti-bacterial crema? Uh, noa. Can ita waita?" he says in his lilting Italian accent. But Bill can't wait and Walter has to descend and put a bandage over his blister. Meanwhile, his wife, Heidi, has blisters all over her feet, awful oozing, red, raw blisters, and she apologizes for not keeping up.

Bill does manage to do all the most difficult trails, though with extra help from Walter. He does not let his fear and fragility get in the way of his ego. I remember once hiking in Tasmania with Lynette, accompanied by a guide. We climbed from a rainforest to a snowy tundra in about eight hours, an ascent that stretched us both to the ends of our physical limits. I would stop periodically to wait for Lynette, sometimes turning back short distances to check in. After a few of these retreats, the guide yelled at me, "Never give up altitude!"—a motto for life that Lynette and I remind each other of often. But women give up altitude all the time and the weakest men never do. Bill's incompetence doesn't stop him from reaching the summits, where he has other people take endless photos of him. He makes Heidi carry a bigger and heavier pack to ensure he makes it to the top. At one point I suggest that Lee, Walter, and I split up Heidi's pack because her feet are in such bad shape, and Bill says, "I would help but I don't have room."

FRAGILITY

I did not believe in a war in the mountains.
—Frederic Henry, *A Farewell to Arms*

When you hike through the Dolomites the remnants of World War I are everywhere: barbed-wire fences, trenches, extensive tunnels—one took us ninety minutes to hike through—bunkers, scraps of old tin ration cans, a piece of a leather army boot, and memorial plaques. Walter tells us more soldiers died of cold and falls than were killed in the war. You understand the term folly of war when you think of sending men into these mountains to fight. Ninety minutes in that tunnel, as I felt the bone-chilling cold and saw my breath escaping up the sides of the blasted rock on what was a warm July day, the history of this place began to work its way through my body. How could masculinity not be terribly fragile? No human body is meant to fight in a place like this and words like courage and bravery are linguistic masks that hide the terror that takes up permanent residence in a soldier's nerve endings. I can see Bill clutching onto the metal cables rounding the five-hundred-meter drops, the fear elongating his face, then holding up a fist at the summit; two moments that will never connect in his mind. He will remember only the summit, but his body contains the unacknowledged fear.

My grandfather, who lost his finger in this war, although not in Italy, was in his eighties by the time I was a kid, laying on our couch on Sunday mornings, a drunk, always in the same blue suit with dandruff sprinkled thickly over the lapels. My mom would put a sheet on the couch to protect it from his suspect hygiene. "Remember, your grandfather loves you," he would say when he would startle awake from a hungover snoring slumber as my mom put two sunny-side-up eggs in front of him. He had been on the Western Front, owned a bar, killed a man, beat my grandmother—all those expressions of masculinity had oozed out over a lifetime and this is what remained, his hair still a wispy blonde. But nothing was left behind those fading blue Italian eyes.

Traveling with men is complicated. It makes me crazy and I love it. This doubling is beginning to be more bearable, holding two truths in a fragile balance. I can enjoy my masculinity and the anonymity of traveling as a man, and I can know that I experience the world and inhabit it with the perspective of a trans man. I love traveling with Lee, a man I admire. He has a small plot in a local community garden. He has always found some patch in Brooklyn to grow flowers and food. He has been a member of the famous Park Slope Food Coop for as long as I can remember. He can't miss a shift or he gets kicked out. We've planned a lot of meals and theater around his shift. During the trip, his longtime partner is having a rough go of it, and I can hear him whispering encouragement in a sweet, soothing tone. Lee challenges me to be a better man: "You don't get to joke anymore about the cleavage of the innkeeper, buddy." I view Lee as a man on a stricter course toward goodness than I am. His politics are less topsy-turvy. I get distracted by the trappings of capitalism, with my sneaker collection and name-brand machismo, a little too easily. Lee would prefer to own one pair of shoes that he would get resoled year after year. He will always buy the cheese on sale. He gives me a hard time, pushing me to make sense of all the contradictions. We both like traveling as men. Neither of us consider telling anyone we're trans. Traveling as trans men is dangerous, and traveling as men is about safety and it's about being able to be ourselves, not a curiosity. Our biggest challenge on the hike is our bladders. Nothing is more defined by gender than the art of peeing on a trail. Women find a place to hide and squat and men whip out their dicks pretty much anywhere and take a whiz. If Lee and I are found squatting, the whole trip will be up for grabs. The Dolomites afford very little cover, few trees, little grass. We stand watch for each other, but like many trans men who like to hike and climb, we hold it for a really long time.

THE SUMMIT

I think I summited my first mountains on this trip. I have hiked a lot and been on top of things before but I don't think I have ever climbed a mountain. This kind of climb requires a coordination of head, body, and heart that is very new to me. At every turn of the climb, you think you are closer than you are. "Are we there yet?" I feel like a kid in the back seat of my parents' car impatiently waiting to arrive somewhere, to just get there. But you can't just get there. In fact, climbing at high altitudes requires the opposite mindset, a present tense, to be in sync with each step—breathe in, lift your legs with purpose so as not to stumble, and land on the bend of your knee gently but firmly. This is what you feel when you walk behind our guide, Walter, a kind of wholeness of being where the flesh of the body moves in sync with the sun, wind, rock, snow, and incline. You cannot distinguish dolomite from boot, legs from gravity, nor the curve of the foot's arch from distance traveled. All I can seem to do is watch Walter move, try to imitate this effortless flow of a body at ease with conditions that are anything but easy. After sharing the "don't give up altitude" story with Walter, he sees me struggling to get down a steep descent where rock has washed away the trail and my only choice is to slide down the mountain. I go low onto my butt to relieve some of the pressure on my knees, and Walter shouts back, "Carl! Don't give up evolution!" I burst out laughing and pull myself to my feet and gingerly slide my way down. The Dolomites make it easy to forget how to stay upright. Lee told me I do the opposite of what a climber should. I speed up during the uphill and slow down when the terrain evens out for a bit. I always push harder when things feel hard.

> But he was fighting in terrain that exposed the flaws in
> this doctrine with utter ruthlessness.
> —The White War

My body vacillates between sitting down to protect itself from falling and plowing through full speed ahead. The doctrine that almost cost the Italians the war, "frontal infantry offensive," espoused by Italian general Luigi Cadorna, resulted in the death of upward of twenty thousand men in the first month of fighting in the Dolomites. The Italian soldiers were ordered to run straight into the enemy fire of the Austrians, who, aided by the Germans, were hidden right inside the walls of the Dolomites in tunnels. Rather than change tactics, Cadorna randomly killed Italian officers who were either advising against his strategy or were unsuccessful in carrying it out. Cadorna's unsubstantiated conviction about mountain warfare led to the worst defeat ever suffered by an Italian army at the Battle of Caporetto. This is the point in the war that drives the narrative of Hemingway's *A Farewell to Arms*, a novel I had studied but never understood until now. The narrator, Frederic Henry, a devoted American lieutenant voluntarily serving in the Italian army, barely escapes his own execution during Cadorna's purge of innocent officers. Had the British and French not come to their aid, the Italians would not have recovered. I am not a military historian, but I understand how men's minds work. They get set on something, and facts and intelligence and dissenting opinions will never override their certainty. I think this is why I am still alive. It would be easy to assume that my body has been on the defensive this entire time. Yes, I have lived in bunkers of terror just trying to survive. I have sat down in psych wards, and on the ledge of bridges. I have feared my father and the many men who have bullied, abused, and neglected me. But I recognize in myself a masculine conviction, one I have always possessed. I will speed up under the most challenging circumstances. When the topography gets steeper, I don't stop to reassess, I push ahead to be able to say I made it to the top, whatever the consequences.

I relate to Bill's blather and bombast. In fact, when I was living as a woman, we had a lot in common. I would talk in hyperbole about my own accomplishments, and overstate my physical capacity. This led to skiing and bike accidents that led to shoulder, hip, and knee surgeries. I used to hike ahead of Lynette, like in Tasmania. I always took the aisle seat on the plane because I needed to be comfortable more than she did. I organized my work schedule and work travel as if my career goals took precedence over hers. Because I was perceived as a woman, these behaviors had consequences from the men they threatened, but I would usually upright myself in order to still make it to the summit. Traveling as a man with other men reveals to me the pitfalls of my own masculinity. The trenches and bunkers in my life have made it hard for me to see the threatening power of my masculine conviction. Polly and Carl make a good team on this trip, watching and learning from their pasts, building a connection to each other.

As Lee and I hike far ahead of our traveling companions, we talk at length about our families. He can't believe that my father left me alone in an emergency room at thirteen. He has his own stories about his complicated relationship with his mother, and as two men in our fifties now, we wonder about how to escape emotional bunkers. We are summiting to our last hut of the trip. Like every approach to a respite in the Dolomites, we are hiking straight uphill. Our hut looks closer than it is. I ask him, "If your mother needed you to clean her private parts, could you do it?" I cannot reconcile walking away from my father and his illness. "I think I could if I had to," he replies.

"That's what I thought, too. I did it, but I couldn't handle it."

"But isn't it time to move on?" he says. "You can't keep going over this forever."

The war betrays Frederic Henry in *A Farewell to Arms*. He never questions his loyalties, his commitment to the fight, until suddenly he finds himself about to be executed for that commitment and he jumps in a river to escape. "It was not my show anymore . . . I would eat and stop thinking. I would have to stop." Yes, I would have to stop, too. The fight with my father isn't my fight anymore. "I wished them all the luck," Henry says of his fellow soldiers. Yes, I wish my father all the luck, but it can't be my show. I won't give up altitude. I am not sure if this is masculine conviction, defensive entrenchment, or a healthy form of survival. The trip provides me a panoramic view. Bill, Walter, Lee, my grandfather, my father. My understanding of the war inside me is shifting—the metaphor of death and despair losing its hold over me as I think more about training and readiness to face what's ahead.

On the last night of the trip Lee and I are in Pisa in a little hotel in the countryside. It's scorching hot, the landscape turned from gray limestone to orange terra-cotta. We are sitting on our hotel room balcony eating a pizza and drinking Italian beer. I feel more and more like a trans man. We are looking at pictures. The pictures from the trip have been the best part of the climb for me. I keep seeing myself. In two years I have become the person I always imagined myself to be. Lee and I have become ourselves together over the years. I remember how depressed he was before his transition; he knows the history of every medication I have ever taken to try to stay alive. These photos of Lee and me make me know there is a future ahead, even though the world is screaming otherwise most days. My favorite photo captures us at the top of Monte Paterno, his right arm raised, my left arm raised as well, holding on to each other, despite so many odds, two trans men at the top of the world.

CHAPTER ELEVEN

TRUTHS

BOSTON

But the most difficult thing for a human being to do is to think ahead, to put ourselves in the shoes of those we have not been yet.
—Hélène Cixous, *Three Steps on the Ladder of Writing*

There is, it seems, no mechanism in the mind or the brain for ensuring the truth, or at least the veridical character, of our recollections. We have no direct access to historical truth, and what we feel or assert to be . . . depends as much on our imagination as our senses.
—Oliver Sacks, "Speak, Memory," *The New York Review of Books*

After finishing a swim at the gym, Lynette texts, "Call me." I know immediately something must be wrong; she never wants to talk on the phone. "I have uterine cancer," she says, her voice trembling. She had a biopsy that the doctor wasn't concerned about and to the doctor's surprise and ours, it's stage-one uterine cancer. There is all kinds of good news in this bad diagnosis. Surgery will "cure" it, the doctor tells us, and he says confidently, "It's my favorite kind of cancer diagnosis. It's slow-growing, and rarely spreads when you catch it early like this." I am relieved by what he is saying and perhaps too practical. I take the doctor at his word. I know a lot of women who have had hysterectomies, and I'm not freaked out by the word cancer. I know cancer has context and the doctor has given us a reassuring one. But I don't have cancer, Lynette does. My thought process doesn't anticipate all the ways in which this diagnosis will begin a new chapter in our marriage. After months of healing, finally beginning to plan a future together again, a hysterectomy throws us backward, into another round of excavating the past, who we were and who we are now. It's like we are transitioning anew or realizing the healing was only a flimsy scab with an oozing and nearly mortal wound still lurking below.

We meet with Lynette's surgeon and he is using words such as cervix, ovaries, vagina, vaginal bleeding, uterus. I know all these words. I still have all of these body parts. I have put my legs in stirrups and had a Pap smear many times. When I had an MRI of my hip several years ago, the male doctor called me at work one day, "Umm, well I am calling because, well umm, when we did the MRI, well you see, we also found, you know, a cyst, in your, umm left ovary. These are common, but you might want to check it out." I was speaking to a leading orthopedic doctor in the city of Chicago and I might as well have been talking to my sixteen-year-old nephew. He couldn't say cyst or ovary. I hung up the phone and forgot the call immediately. It was a conversation that disappeared into my body, a body preferring to risk sickness or death rather than have a vaginal ultrasound. But hearing Lynette's diagnosis, the list of *her* body parts, is easy for me to track. I am not listening to Lynette's doctor thinking I have a uterus still. I have *never* thought about my uterus. Rather, I am listening as her husband, a steady hand, a good man who will do whatever she needs.

Then the fights between us begin immediately. They are fresh and raw. This cancer, a cancer of the uterus, splits Lynette open to the feelings of me as a man in her life, a man she is supposed to depend on to be by her side. Within a day of getting the news, she sobs to me, "It's different now. I'm all alone." If I hadn't transitioned, she says, we would have been two women in this together. Would we have? She stirs a flurry of resentment against me as she begins talking to all her female friends about how it feels to be sixty-three and losing what makes her a woman, and to be doing it accompanied by some man she doesn't even know. A rage bubbles up inside her. I know this rage. It's the rage I saw in the cemetery the day I told Lynette I would change my gender marker. It's the rage I felt in our bed after my first testosterone shot. It's the rage that keeps floating up the stairs every time she walks down into the basement and unseals a box of our history and finds invitations to my fortieth birthday party or her fiftieth, when she flips through vacation photos in Italy and Ireland and Tasmania and Japan. Especially when she sees the photos from our wedding party. Polly is everywhere in that basement, and so is our lesbian past. "I didn't sign up for this"—six words that have been said many times before, but have taken on new meaning. "I miss Polly," she cries to Barbara, our couples' therapist who we see right after the diagnosis. The dead name startles me. I am pissed that she is clinging to Polly again.

Like a man, I am oblivious to the stakes of the diagnosis and to Lynette's rage taking on new proportions. I don't think I would have responded any differently pretransition. I didn't feel like a woman then. In the rare moments I have thought about my female anatomy, it's only to consider how to make it disappear. I yearned for my mother's breast cancer to be the genetic kind so I could have a preventive double mastectomy, and was disappointed when she called me gleefully to tell me it wasn't. I don't anticipate Lynette's rage coming at me, and I make a terrible joke: "Maybe the doctor would do a twofer," I say as we leave the surgeon's office. I would love to get rid of the body parts she is clinging to. I don't have a clue what it feels like to inhabit her body even though in a biology class-room way our bodies still have plenty in common. Binaries mean everything and nothing in these moments. The binary of what remains of our shared women's anatomy still does not allow me to inhabit what Lynette feels like as a woman losing her uterus. The binary that makes me a man in this situation brings a truth home to Lynette's body that we thought we had faced but hadn't.

Her friends advise her not to confide in me about the grief she feels losing a part of her womanhood. "Don't reveal that kind of vulnerability to a man," they tell her. "Intimacy between men and women is different." Though she isn't sup-posed to talk to me, they ask her repeatedly, "Where's Carl? Is he going to be at the hospital during the surgery?" "If Carl doesn't step up, I'll fly there and take care of you." A few days after the surgery, they ask, "Where's Carl been? Is he helping you? Feeding you?"

Was I formed out of the air two years ago, a man who landed in my house with a wife and no history? I have been with Lynette twenty years. She has cancer. She is having sur-gery. Where else would I be, man or woman? One friend tells Lynette that when she had her hysterectomy her husband went to work the next day and left her with their three dogs. She was unable to go and up down the stairs to get to the bathroom. Another friend tells her there was no one around to drive her home after her hysterectomy. This friend has been married thirty years. Did these women think I had become their husbands? These are queer women and liberal women and women of color and white women, all saying the same thing: "No man can understand what you're going through." Some small part of my outrage is tempered as I consider what parts of what they are saying are true. How can my body hold multiple truths in this unanticipated circumstance, when a body faces death, a health crisis, or a loss of freedom; are there only women and men? I am jolted into a very particular version of "husband" by the women around Lynette and this is where being a trans man is different from being born with a penis, at least for me. I may not feel what Lynette is feeling, but I have spent my entire life around women, in love with women, performing as a daughter, sister, and lesbian lover. How could anyone think I don't know how to care for Lynette, especially Lynette? Once again Lynette and I face the life-and-death moment when a gender marker, hers this time, is removed from a body—the precipice on which our marriage continues to sit.

What truth about me is more true now? How different am I from my wife? Is testosterone the line between loneliness and togetherness?

As we fight, I start to feel more like an asshole guy—pushed into the position of bad husband by all the assumptions that I am already there. I have fought so hard to be seen as a man, and it's as if everyone has now forgotten I'm a trans man. I didn't see this coming.

> *Under the blow of the truth, the eggshell we are breaks.*
> *Right in the middle of life's path: the apocalypse; we*
> *lose a life.*
> —Hélène Cixous, *Three Steps on the Ladder of Writing*

Lynette and I get into a truth war about her illness and my transition and we break each other like eggshells. It's all coming out. One truth about a gender transition is that more people are concerned about the spouse than the person going through the transition. A spouse is the victim of a seemingly irrational choice. Lynette clings to this truth in a whole new way and she feels owed for what's happened to her, for what I've done to her. She tells me everything she needs to get through the cancer: touch, no bad jokes, and please text her several times a day, "I love you, I am with you, and it will be okay." I am furious. I know exactly what she needs, it's what I wanted these last two years when she refused to touch me, refused to tell me that it would be okay. As we fight she cries, "Your transition tore my skin off. I wish we had separated the minute you started taking testosterone." This is a new truth I haven't heard. She is accessing two years of anger inside her own terror. I start making a list of my truths in my head, all the shit people felt they had to say to me, everything I've endured.

> "Do you have a cold?"
> "No, I'm fine, thanks, the voice-dropping is part of the transition."
> "Well you sound like you have cold."
> "What do you think of my beard?"
> "I think they call that scruff."
> "I thought you were doing this transition thing the last time we talked."
> "I'm interested in the poor wife, what about her story?"
> "I hate that haircut. I hate your beard. I hate your sneakers. I can't touch you."

Those last truths are from Lynette. I may have blunted them a little. My response to Lynette's needs is self-centered, steeped in a desire for retribution. I am ready to share some of my truths. I tell Lynette during one argument that "Yes, I wish I were single now." I want to be single and soak in a life for the first time with no expectations, no responsibilities to anyone but myself. I want to talk to people as me. I want to travel like Anthony Bourdain did, to parts unknown. I want to know if women would be attracted to me. I want to flirt and have someone discover me sexually for the first time and yearn for my body, this one, not the one in the boxes in the basement. We are feeling each other now, Lynette and me. Her suspicion of and general dislike of men and my restlessness and curiosity for everything new and fresh and male are being replayed as if it's 2016.

Lynette and I have opposite narratives about the last two years. I abandoned her. She abandoned me.

I have read and heard stories of marriages that dissolve when someone gets sick. I was in the psych ward once with a woman who drove to work one morning, had a psychotic break, landed in the hospital, and while she was there, her girlfriend of ten years left her and took their house. "Who does this?" I remember saying to Lynette during visiting hours one night. I get it now. I know exactly how it happens. Vulnerability and terror create the most unpredictable circumstances.

These are the most horrible weeks of our marriage. We both feel terrible. We are both afraid. We both wonder if we came this far and now have to admit that we didn't make it. Our marriage is close to over. She tells me to stop making her cancer about me. But she made my becoming me all about her. I feel childish when I type that sentence, recognizing its tit-for-tat sensibility.

I know a gender transition and cancer aren't the same. Relationships are irrational. Truth is nuanced. I don't think of being transgender as a sickness that you get out of the blue. I do think about it as a condition of a body that requires treatment, long-term support, and a careful relationship to truth. When Lynette gets cancer, it's a terrible thing that has happened to her because it is. Everyone already knows this. I transition by some twisted version of choice and I am held accountable for truths of my own making. Could you imagine saying to someone in the midst of cancer treatment, "When will this whole cancer thing be over? When will you be in remission or when will you be dead?" It doesn't matter if a person who has had chemo looks better or worse bald; we know to say "You look amazing." Comparisons don't need to be precise or logical. This comparison with Lynette's cancer lives in my body, it's how my body felt in the first few weeks of her illness—torn between my fierce love for her and my own pain over our lost connection, over all the judgments that come with a transition that would never be spoken aloud with a cancer diagnosis.

There are different kinds of terror and vulnerability, but everything Lynette is saying about how she feels and what she needs provokes a truth from my mouth and my body that makes me sound like and feel like a terrible person: "Yeah, now you know how I felt."

———————

I haven't heard much about how my dad is doing with his cancer. It's been two months since we have been in communication, though he texts me that he's heard Lynette has cancer and to give her his best. Two cancer diagnoses for two family members in five months' time. More truths than I know what to do with—again sorting past from present and retribution from trauma and self-preservation from cruelty.

I must contend with the list of truths my body feels.

My father had been lying about his gambling habit to us for more than a decade, saying as recently as a few months ago, "I haven't gambled in twelve years." Except my brother looked at his taxes and they tell another story. This means there is no money for his care or my mom's.

My father watched my mother's mental decline and kept reporting to us that working fifty hours a week was good for her. My brothers and I knew after going through her files, talking to her colleagues, and seeing the severity of her decline that her income had been necessary for him to keep his golf club membership and his card playing intact.

I miss texting with him about the Cubs and Notre Dame football. I am watching a slew of football documentaries I want to tell him about.

He sends me J.Crew gift cards every Christmas.

One time he visited Minneapolis and realized we only had one frying pan and bought us an expensive cast iron pancake griddle.

I fundamentally believe he did the best he could as a

father. I believe most people do what they can no matter how big they fail.

When I am around my father I lose track of myself. He has become his worst self in this illness. The sound of his rage and fear from his hospital bed or his TV recliner fill me with the memories of him chasing me down the street to spank me, hitting me with his leather belt on my bare bottom, stopping the car on the highway when I was twenty-three to punch me repeatedly for swearing. All the terror and vulnerability. My body cannot text him back, call him, or send him a card right now. This doesn't feel good, but it's true.

As my grandmother, diagnosed schizophrenic in her eighties, an immigrant who never recovered from that trauma, became more paranoid, delusional, and mean to everyone who visited, my mother quit speaking to her. I begged my mother to end her silence. "She's sick, Mom. She's all alone. She is old. She needs us." My mother wouldn't budge, my twenty-year-old self could not believe my social worker mother would abandon hers. I wonder if she wished she were single, with no children? She put a magnet on our refrigerator when we were young: "Raising kids is like being pecked to death by chickens." Eventually she visited my grandmother as she was dying. My grandmother rambled on about my aunt, the saint, who came to visit her every day. My mother would call me and rant, "I took care of her my whole life and your aunt shows up for four weeks and *she's* the saint?" What truths was she harboring?

I tried to save my mom from my father when I was in my early thirties and Lynette and I had been together for a few years. This was a year or two after my mom had abandoned me at the therapist's office. I still hadn't given up on us. She flew to Minneapolis right before the robocalls started twenty years ago. Lynette and I took her to dinner and theater and museums. She complained about my dad's gambling, her unhappiness, his inability to change, the terrible way he talked to her. She admitted for the hundredth time she wanted to leave him, words I had heard since my early childhood. We talked about her coming to live with us in Minneapolis. We would help her get licensed and set up a therapy practice. We laughed and planned. I couldn't think of anything I wanted more than for her to live nearby, for us to be close again like we had been during those few years of high school and through college. I thought Lynette and I had convinced her. A few days after that trip, she called me and said, "I will never travel to Minneapolis without your father again." I never had another meaningful conversation with my mother. She hunkered down with him. Now seeing the shell of what was left of her in the visits home—the film of dust over every surface except the kitchen counter that she wipes and wipes. The anxious, repetitive questioning: What are we doing now? What are we doing now? The recasting of history, my dad as a devoted father—I knew that we would never reunite after his death, something I had fantasized about. She was gone. Another devastating truth.

———————

Who teaches us to hold multiple truths side by side? Is this the primary work of parents or teachers or coaches? I never learned this skill, until now, transitions like dreams forcing us into places with no warning or preparation. I am learning to sort truths and make decisions that aren't clear or obvious but live in gradations of nuanced emotion. This is the hardest work of my life, the most difficult part of a marriage. My body feels so many things and my brain is slow to comprehend. I had always thought that my brain was the quickest and most efficient part of me, but I have learned that it's my body that knows everything first.

> *Love and the axe are inseparable. Only the ones who love us can kill us.*
> —Hélène Cixous, *Three Steps on the Ladder of Writing*

At the moment of Lynette's diagnosis she treats me like a man, like the worst men she has ever known. It is me and it's not me, it's all the men sitting in the White House right now, all the men trying to end reproductive freedom; Brett Kavanaugh; all the men she has carefully made a life to avoid. But I am also all the men that she has loved, like her father and my brothers. Her body holds multiple truths about me and about men. Her diagnosis takes us to Cixous's moment of the axe in our story together: only those we love can kill us. We are figuring out how not to kill each other, how not to let the axe fall permanently on our life together.

Lynette is healing. I am caring for her. Before the diagnosis and surgery we had been planning to live together in Berlin for the fall. We wonder if we should separate and if I should go alone, but we know that will likely be a permanent goodbye. We decide to move ahead with our plans, to refuse to give up on our marriage. We have moved together so many times. Our first big move as a couple was from a home I owned to a house we bought together. That move happened during a stretch of ninety-degree days in July. The day before the movers came, I was running around in boxers and a T-shirt in a flop sweat in our little tiny home without air-conditioning, packing this box, and patching that wall, and scheduling the final walk-through with the buyers. I ran up the stairs to grab something and found Lynette on the office floor, pictures spread out, making photo albums. I looked on in disbelief. "Photo albums are something you make on a cold winter night in front of a fire, drinking hot chocolate, not a project to start eighteen hours before we move!" We have laughed at this story for almost two decades. She makes me crazy and I love that she was making a photo album, how her mind zeroes in on something and her patience is endless; time is always slower for her. She sends me her premove to-do list from her sick bed. We leave in two weeks, and she is recovering from major surgery, and a house sitter will care for our dogs, and we have a bathroom remodel in process that is in total disarray and on her list: "Send a nice card to so-and-so, send a congratulations card to so-and-so, reorganize the poetry books in the basement." I see the list and I laugh and I feel some huge relief come over my whole body. I love her so much. This is also our history; though not recognizable now in those photographs in the basement, it is the truest truth my body knows: memories of Polly and Lynette that I will always cherish as we keep finding our way to Lynette and Carl. We are still here together because we are holding on to the knowing that multiple truths and bodies are possible.

CHAPTER TWELVE

MAN TALK

EVERYWHERE

You go for a man hard enough and fast enough, he don't have time to think about how many's with him; he thinks about himself, and how he might get clear of that wrath that's about to set down on him.
—John Wayne as Rooster Cogburn, *True Grit*

I like man talk. Lee and Walter and Alex, and Frank, when he was still alive. My friend Corey is twenty-eight and the buddy I always dreamed of having when I was his age—we talk superhero movies and sneakers and clothes and beers and work and relationships and weight-lifting and dogs and politics. I love chatting it up with guys about women and workouts and bourbons. It's not that I don't like to talk literature and opera and art too, but I secretly relish a kind of macho bravado that is still very much a part of barbershops and locker rooms and whiskey bars. As much as I bathe in man talk some days, I know the stunted nature of its evolution.

My father's father painted houses for a living, drank too much for a time, and sat in a recliner and yelled at my grandmother for most of the years I knew him. "Cookie, bring me an iced tea. Cookie, I'm starving, get me a sandwich. Cookie, turn that radio off, I'm watching the game." They fought constantly, she ran around to serve him while he barked orders and moaned, "My legs are bothering me, my sugar's too high, look at the arthritis in that finger." My father's chatter is a replica of his father's; he too reduced to life in his recliner, on oxygen, his partial teeth sitting on the table next to him. The only things he is in control of now are the TV remote and my mother, shouting orders, a one-way man talk I have spent my entire life listening to. My father's masculinity has been shaped by my grandfather's, shaped by poverty, shaped by military service, shaped by bars and poker games and the freedom of not feeling responsible for being home with his children. Men like my father and grandfather—on edge, talking too much, asserting power even when lying on their backs—practice a burned-out masculinity that is still at the center of American life, still the building block of patriarchy.

Some fucked-up part of me wants this sometimes. I was in a Lyft the other night talking to a guy who is trying to join the Navy, to become a dental technician. He tells me he's doing it "for his woman." "I think she's the one," he says tentatively. "They only want your money, and I've told her I haven't got any, but I'm making her sign a prenup anyway." I hear myself say "Yeah, man, I feel you. My wife hasn't worked in like ten years, all that bullshit about women's rights." He starts cracking up, "Yeah, you know, my man, you know what I'm saying." I tip him ten dollars and give him five stars for letting me indulge my inner asshole. That guy talk that I have been trained so well in replicating. I don't beat myself up about these exchanges. My friend Lee tells me it's my job to correct this behavior, and sometimes I do, but sometimes I dive right in, trying to grasp at some false sense of power that I know has been used against me a thousand times in another life. Usually it happens because I've been fighting with Lynette that day and it feels good to talk shit with another guy right before I walk in the house and have to deal with whatever it is we're arguing about.

I think it's hard for people to understand what I mean when I say "I'm a guy's guy." I am in one way "becoming" a man and in another way I have always been one and I'm trying out all the ways to understand how I want to live that out, good and bad. Becoming a white man visibly is like a newly found superpower—like when Spider-Man suddenly realizes he can scale the sides of buildings but doesn't quite know how to control his own power and smashes up against a concrete wall on his first several attempts. He flails until he eventually knows how to use his power for good.

I send Lynette a photo. It's seven men, drinking and eating scattered around a bar in New York City, at least one empty chair between each guy, except for two Irish guys standing together watching a game. The bartender is giving a lengthy lesson on Belgian beers to another guy, one of those way-too-much-detail lectures about yeasts and the fermentation process. "The Lambic Belgians are spontaneously fermented, meaning the wort, that's the liquid extracted from the mashing process, is open to the air, allowing yeasts and bacteria to get into the beer. You're drinking some good bacteria, man." I'm trying to watch the Notre Dame game and listen to the beer talk. I tell the Irish guys that I graduated from Notre Dame, in the Digger Phelps era of coaching. "Wait, when did you graduate then?" one of the guys asks in a thick brogue.

"1988."

"No way, man. How are old are you?"

"Fifty-two, dude."

"I thought you were like thirty maybe, you work out a lot?"

"Yeah, swim, lift, you know."

"Cool, man, next one's on me, bro."

This is how we talk. Lynette sees the picture and texts, "Look at all your boyfriends." She's right. We bond in our solitude, relishing these moments when nobody needs anything from us. The relief of time passing, present tense. Where do women pass time without expectation? Do these men have children at home? Are the children up waiting for them? Are their wives or girlfriends or husbands or boyfriends waiting too? Is man talk in 2018 so different from man talk in 1950? This looks and sounds like a scene out of a film or an evening news report I've watched a thousand times over the decades.

JUST MY RIFLE, PONY, AND ME

John Wayne made the film *Rio Bravo* with director Howard Hawkes in 1959 as a response to Stanley Kramer's 1952 film *High Noon*, starring Gary Cooper. Wayne thought *High Noon* was a statement against blacklisting and McCarthyism, something he fully supported as an icon of American patriotism and masculinity. Whereas Cooper played a conflicted protagonist, torn between his pacifist wife and his responsibility to stop a vicious outlaw, Wayne's character in *Rio Bravo*, John T. Chance, suffers no inner conflict about his responsibilities as sheriff. Wayne explains to Roger Ebert in a 1969 interview after the release of *True Grit*, that the western

> . . . *can be understood in every country. The good guys against the bad guys. No nuances. And the horse is the best vehicle of action in our medium. You take action, a*

*scene, and scenery, and cut them together, and you never
miss. Action, scene, scenery.*

Wayne might be single-handedly responsible for taking
nuance out of masculinity in America, reducing it to guns
and horses and cocky man talk. My brother Tim used to imitate Wayne at the dinner table when we were kids. For about
a year, every time he sat down he would mime tipping his
cowboy hat and say, "Well, listen pilgrim and listen tight . . ."
When my father became ill, he told us to take anything from
the house we wanted. The only thing I took was a drawing
Tim made in the eighth grade, a one-color pencil drawing of
John Wayne in a cowboy hat that he gave to my father as a
Christmas present. No nuances.

When talking with men, I sometimes feel as if I am in a
John Wayne movie, that our language to express masculinity
hasn't evolved that much: "This is my rifle from *Stagecoach*,"
he tells Ebert in the interview. "One of the kind you could
spin like this. . . .

"Jesus, I wrecked that shoulder. Down in Baton Rouge,
when I was making *The Undefeated* I twisted around in the
saddle and the damn stirrup was completely loose. I fell right
under that goddamned horse; I'm lucky I didn't kill myself."

I have had this exact same conversation in the locker room
about shoulders and bike crashes and guns. Once with an

emergency room doctor on crutches in the locker room after he had managed an upper body workout. "Yeah, I fractured my hip; my bike and I flew right over this car that turned in front of me, smashed his windshield. But I'll be back on the bike in a month or so." He grins.

"Totally been there, bro, I flew over my handlebars going full speed down a hill in Maine, dislocated my shoulder," and I proceed to show him the huge road rash scar still visible under my right elbow.

A man and his horse, a man and his bike, a man and his car, a man and his gun, a man and his Belgian beers, a man and his whiskey. As Dean Martin and Ricky Nelson sing in a favorite moment in *Rio Bravo*:

> *Just my rifle, pony, and me*
> *Just my rifle, my pony, and me*

In 1981, then president of Mexico José López Portillo gifted President Ronald Reagan a white Arabian horse named El Alamein. Another American movie star cowboy, Reagan would say repeatedly, "There is nothing quite so good for the inside of a man as the outside of a horse," a line people thought was his but actually came from the Greek soldier Xenophon's *The Art of Horsemanship*, written in the fourth or fifth century BC. You have likely seen the photo of Vladimir

Putin from his August 2009 vacation in Siberia in which he is riding shirtless on his horse—a "beefcake" shot, accompanied by others where he is in camouflage and one where, as the journalist Nick Hayes writes, he is "propelling himself through the water by a power breaststroke." The truest moment of tenderness and vulnerability in the HBO series *The Sopranos* comes when Tony Soprano falls in love with the horse Pie-O-My. In the forty-fourth episode the horse falls sick, and as she lies on her side, he rubs her head, lights a cigar, a goat enters the stable bleating, and Tony smiles. He settles in next to Pie-O-My as the rain falls outside the stable and we hear Dean Martin singing "My Rifle, My Pony, and Me" in *Rio Bravo*. Who needs men to even talk when a horse is in the picture?

The image I will never get out of my head is former Alabama senator Roy Moore, accused of multiple counts of sexual misconduct, riding his horse, Sassy, into Gallant, Alabama, to vote for himself in his 2017 race against Doug Jones. The best part of his failed tough guy performance was not just that he lost the election but that he exposed the fact that he had no idea how to ride a horse, as Horse Twitter was afire with all his mistakes—the stirrups were too long, the bridle was adjusted improperly, his legs jutted unnaturally in front of him. When you think masculinity can't look more foolish, there's always some guy willing to ride in on a horse and prove you wrong.

I am understanding my relationship to westerns differently now. I am rethinking my own man talk, well, at least some of the time. I see what drew my father to these films, and what drew me to them. It's a relief to avoid complexity; it can be done from a recliner with a remote control in hand. It's a twisted convalescence that makes you sicker, but the point is to get away permanently, not to heal but to escape, to believe in a clarity about living that doesn't exist. I understand my father so much more now, the way he learned to channel some of his rage and violence into a screen of fantasy where men are men and women are women and the bad guys usually get their due. If you think of the history of narratives about men, it's strangely difficult to think of ones that reflect nuance and tenderness, which is what made *Moonlight*, for example, the 2016 film written and directed by Barry Jenkins, based on a play written by Tarell Alvin McCraney, such an incredible step forward in imagining masculinity, in this case black masculinity.

Chloé Zhao's 2018 film *The Rider* gives us a new story about men, prairies, and horses. She asks us to consider what a man does when the only thing he has been trained to do is taken away from him. When the only story he knows must be rewritten. It is a fresh look at man talk, horses, and destinations for masculinity. The film is set in South Dakota, in the heart of hypermasculine rodeo culture as lived by a group of Lakota Sioux men on the Pine Ridge Reservation. Zhao has seamlessly woven documentary and fiction, a part-true and part-made-up account of the real-life story of Brady Jandreau, who plays himself in the film, but with a different surname. In the film, Brady fractures his skull in a bad fall from a bronco and almost dies. He is told he can never ride again.

In an early scene in the film, Brady is asleep and sick in his cramped bedroom in the family's small trailer, having left the hospital too soon. His three buddies show up, blow cigarette smoke into his face, and drag him out of bed. They go off together to smoke weed and drink as they wander at sunset through the open and beautifully filmed expanse of the reservation. Later, they sit around a fire and share rodeo war stories: "I had ten-plus concussions; by NFL standards I should be dead." They want to know when Brady is going to man up and ride again: "You don't let pain put you down, you ain't gonna be turning out horses left and right just because your head hurts a little bit now, are ya?"

"I'm not drawing out of anything, a head's a little bit different than ribs," Brady says to buy himself time. "It's all the same for a cowboy, ride through the pain," his friend insists.

Brady hears some version of "a man always gets back on

his horse" from rodeo fans at the checkout counter in the supermarket where he takes a job to make ends meet, as well as from his friends and his family. But Brady's body is telling him otherwise; he is having seizures, and the smallest jolt could kill him. The scene around the fire is in one sense the most familiar man talk: all the injuries the guys have accrued, and then nostalgic memories of their friend Lane. Lane was once the best rider on the reservation and is now paralyzed with brain damage and in a wheelchair at a rehab center. They laugh together about Lane's womanizing, how he used to say "One thing I learned in life, [I] always thought girls come in with a name and leave with a number." "That dirty dog," they chuckle. But something about the scene differentiates it from a John Wayne film; there's nuance here. When the laughing stops, the guys hold hands and pray for their brother Lane: "We are him and he is us, we are all one in this together." This early moment in the film presages an unexpected and refreshing take on the ways men talk.

Complex stories of humanity combined with our capacity for imagination are what give us hope. This is why I make art, it's why despite wanting to die at different points in my life, I believe I am still here. Hope for me, for this trans guy, has been extremely hard to come by, and it's always the stories of books and films and theater that I hold on to. Not unlike the film *Thelma & Louise*, a film that was the center of my graduate school dissertation, a film I loved for its dirty feminine toughness, *The Rider* made me feel some glimmer of a fresh narrative possibility for masculinity. It's not the first film to show men being sweet with horses, not the first film to show men caring for one another, but it felt like a film America needed in 2018.

There are two scenes that will stay with me as I keep exploring how Carl and Polly make a man, how we find a language that fits. The first is Brady with an Arabian thoroughbred. "Nobody has ever been on his back, nobody has ever touched him," the owner who has hired Brady to break the horse tells him. It's a four-minute scene that I could watch go on forever. The horse bucks and runs and settles, bucks and runs and settles. Then he receives his first human touch as Brady rubs his nose, then his hindquarters. Around they go in circles, Brady with a rope, pulling the horse forward, two steps at a time. Brady throws his body perpendicular, chest down over the horse's back "to teach him pressure." "Trust, trust," he whispers. In the final image, he is sitting atop the horse. We have not witnessed a victory or a conquering, but a love scene, a man who knows innately how connection happens, how we traverse emotional distance, how we calm one another's fears.

Similarly, toward the end of the film, Brady goes to visit Lane. He is wearing his cowboy hat, green rodeo shirt, jeans, and a bandanna tied around his neck as if he's ready to go riding. With the help of the nurses at the rehab facility, he dresses Lane in boots, jeans, and his old maroon-striped rodeo shirt. Brady puts Lane's cowboy hat atop his head: "We don't want you to get a sunburn," he says. With great difficulty, they ease Lane over a saddle propped up on parallel bars. Brady holds the reins as if he is the horse and takes Lane riding again. "You're loping off into the distance," he says as Lane struggles to stay upright. Lane's head falls and Brady cajoles it back up with the patience of a parent teaching a child to ride a bike. Together they are in a rehab facility loping, smiling, tilting, riding, Brady talking softly, lovingly. Brady's man talk soothes me. I have been the horse and I have been Lane, broken through a transition, learning to allow my body to feel pressure, to be cajoled to walk two steps forward, to trust someone enough to help me imagine what it would be like to lope along in my cowboy hat protecting me from sunburn, to learn what it means to talk like a man.

CHAPTER THIRTEEN

DESTINATIONS

BERLIN, GERMANY

Everyone has a self-made pass for travel through the terror and sadness of the world, and because, in the end, nothing is sufficient, everyone wants to share his own method, hoping for strength in numbers.
—Mark Helprin, *A Soldier of the Great War*

am convalescing. Rest and lakeside breezes and crisp fall air, two years into my manhood I realize Polly and Carl keep interrupting each other, telling parallel and sometimes conflicting stories. I am in a place that is like a sanitarium. My meals are cooked for me and my apartment is cleaned once a week. I do not speak the language, nothing interrupts my rest. I am apart from the daily realities of American life. I am so far away that not even the Presidential Alert texted to every American tonight can reach me. I am resting and healing and accountable only to Lynette. We are healing together. A trans body needs time. A disrupted marriage needs time.

Convalescence, a term that comes from the Latin *convalescere*: "to grow fully strong." We are not a country that values a healthy citizenry, the fight over affordable healthcare is an example that proves a lot of Americans think some people deserve to be sick and saddled with medical bills they will never be able to pay. If they die because they couldn't afford their insulin, it's their own fault for not better accessing the opportunities afforded by the American dream. Many men in America cannot imagine that a woman can still feel an assault forty years after the fact. How many women need a sanitarium after 2018, the year of misogyny, yet another year of misogyny?

Lynette's grandmother went to a sanitarium, the J. N. Adams Sanitarium in Perrysburg, New York, which opened in 1912, after her daughter died of influenza in the early 1920s at the age of three or four. She went to convalesce from the grief of such an astounding loss. The sanitarium was primarily for tuberculosis patients; it was where the Swiss had been proving that the fresh air, known as the "sunshine cure," for TB patients actually worked. The hospital was also used to treat traumas and other kinds of illnesses that might benefit from a change of scenery. Like most sanitariums, it is abandoned now. Lynette and I visited it several years ago. The property and its surroundings are serene, and the buildings, though empty and crumbling, were created to be a magical site of healing, a large dining hall with a spectacular domed roof, a large kitchen area, the hospital located on a remote hillside surrounded by forest. It was a moment in our history that seems impossible now, the idea that healthcare should be humane and comfortable and patients should be given the time they need to grow strong. America's specialty is day surgeries. In and out, "It won't be too painful," the orthopedic doctor tells me after major shoulder surgery, the pain so excruciating my first night home that I can't imagine how I will live through the night. In one local county journal from Perrysburg, the question is posed, "Where would our region be were it not for the thousands of our citizens who were healed there and went on to shape Buffalo and western New York?" There is a profound recognition that each life strengthened mattered to a community and its future. With each day I am stronger now. I am not suicidal. I am not afraid to look back, and I know that every step forward requires that I embrace both parts of myself, that I don't fall into a masculine wholeness that demands forgetting.

I am living in Wannsee on the outer edge of the southwestern part of Berlin. There is a heaviness here despite the calming environs that requires not forgetting. No convalescence is ever without history and context. The River Havel sits outside my apartment window where I watch the flapping white sails of boats from the yacht club next door slide across the water. The sun sets pink and purple every evening. This is the same river that is in view from inside the House of the Wannsee Conference, where, in 1942, fifteen high-ranking Nazi leaders met to discuss "The Final Solution of the Jewish Question." The meeting took place only a fifteen-minute walk away from where I am resting. It is the most frightening place I have ever visited. There is a map inside the mansion that tallies all the Jews in Europe by country; the goal was to exterminate eleven million. The photos of the white male Nazis who attended the conference posted along a steel fence on my way into the house make me physically ill. I can't stay in this space for long. I walk around the grounds; there is no setting more elegant—the juxtaposition between the evil that took place inside the conference room walls and the beauty of the water and the trees and the peacefulness of its surroundings is often noted.

I am watching the news back home—more prominent white men being dismissed from their jobs for years of sexual misconduct, a black man just shot and killed in his own apartment. Are American leaders headed into a conference room like the one down the street from me? The air in America is so thick with white supremacy, misogyny, immigration atrocities, and transphobia. I get an email from a Muslim friend; he is writing about debt and sends me an article in which he calls out identity politics as a smoke screen for creating an economy that enslaves people to debt. We offer the false promise of borrowing to get us somewhere else, the false promise of American mobility is why we are where we are, he argues. My goddaughter has seventy thousand dollars in student loan debt. Will the fact that she's female, or brown, or that she owes determine her future as she leaves her two-year service rotation in the Peace Corps?

The time it takes to transition a life, just a single life. We know there is never enough time to transition a country to become its best self. The shock of living through this time is feeling all the ways that people do not change, do not want you to change, and do not want the very thing they have pledged since their earliest school days, right hand over their heart: "liberty and justice for all."

I am thinking a lot about the next generation. I want to believe the students from Stoneman Douglas High School in Parkland, Florida, and their activism and demands for change will move us closer to a more humane and civil society. I want to believe my goddaughter's insistence on service and caring for the lives of every color and gender and ethnicity here and abroad is movement toward a future that will never allow babies to be separated from their parents at a border ever again. I want to believe my sixteen-year-old nephew, who transitioned with me from aunt to uncle without a hiccup, is what is in store for all trans people moving forward. My story is about one trans life. My road to manhood is a single story of survival, though you may want to read it as something bigger. You may want me to stand in for all bodies like mine, except my body is only this body. I read just today that more than half of trans male teens and one-third of all teenagers questioning their gender have attempted suicide. The conversation around transgender lives is youthful, tragic, and still in such early stages of discovery. There are many more stories that must be told for us to even glimpse the history and complexity that trans embodies.

Like any identity category, it's impossible to lump groups of people together by sex organs or skin color or religious affiliation. But we do it anyway as a way to argue for political change and human rights. My friend Robin and I have been fleeing in opposite directions for some time and clinging together in the same struggle. Robin came to me during my transition for advice about how to begin theirs. Assigned male at birth, they had never been comfortable in their body, had always felt "awkward, itchy in their skin." They didn't say, "I think I'm a woman," but rather, "I know this body isn't mine." I help find them a therapist with expertise in treating trans people. I will admit, however, to my own transphobia that infiltrated our first conversation. That day they entered my office, they appeared to be the kind of man I was headed toward becoming—an athletic body, an on-and-off beard, good sneakers; a young person I could imagine myself resembling in a year or so. "Why in God's name," I thought to myself, "would they give up what I want so badly?" Trans is strange that way, one person running toward something another person can't escape fast enough.

Robin's story is one I have heard several times in the last couple of years; unlike me, they don't have a gender marker destination. They use the pronouns they/them and aren't planning to identify as a woman. They kindly take all my curious questions because I don't fully understand what transition means for them. They are taking hormones and having surgeries that will allow them to be more female in appearance. "Why not embrace woman as an identity?" They tell me, "I was probably born a woman, but the category is so saturated in attributes of sweetness and reticence that I don't see in myself. And the way that trans women have been portrayed as hyperfeminine, well, that embarrasses me to think of." If they had to pick a category, they say they hope to resemble some version of butch lesbian, but even that isn't quite right. "Nonbinary is the right word for now." I hear something similar from an acquaintance, Eleanor, who is transitioning. Assigned female at birth, they are taking testosterone, but aren't planning a name change and "would never inhabit the gender male." Again, nonbinary is the term they use. And another young person in the theater industry, assigned female at birth, says, "I'm taking testosterone so I can dress more feminine and express my queerness more visibly." What? What? What?—taking testosterone to be more feminine?

Robin and I talk about queerness. They tell me, "The one thing I've always known is that I'm queer." I, by contrast, say, "I never felt queer," and we laugh together about this crazy word transgender and all that it is holding. And though these experiences are not mine, I love that so many young people are refusing gender categories. "Too much baggage," they tell me. Why shouldn't they refuse to be boxed in? We are part of a history of exploration of what bodies are and can become. Why should our discoveries have predetermined endpoints? Pronouns that suit aren't a privilege everyone is born with.

I cannot enter the feeling of a body that isn't mine. I can only open myself to learning what I don't feel, and believing that even if I don't feel it, it can still be very real. This seems simple, but the people who have come along in my transition are critical and cruel about what my body feels, pissed that in this era of mounting claims of the sexual abuse and harassment of women, that I could dare to feel like a man, or maintaining that anatomy is a predetermined binary expressed in body parts that I shouldn't be allowed to alter—this is a kind of gender hubris, a righteousness that taken to its extreme leads to academic conferences, ballot measures, and political votes that will determine which bodies get to live in peace. The House of the Wannsee Conference looms in my background, the worst of humanity expressed in obsessions about bodies—bloodlines and race, and sex and sexuality—those determined worthy enough to get to live and thrive and those who think they get to decide.

As the very worst of white masculinity in America is hopefully at the beginning stages of gasping its last breath, as a record number of women of every sexuality and color are about to enter Congress, and as my convalescence winds down inside a country that knows white male supremacy in its bones, I realize my time in Berlin has been a roundup of all the good men in my life. Lee came to visit and I cajoled my frugal friend into a pair of Berlin-made sneakers, although there was not an immediate event or need for new sneakers, a miracle that can only be expressed in its own book. My buddy Corey came and we got matching haircuts, drank craft beer, and jumped from mini trampoline to mini trampoline scattered in a small Berlin park. We were boys together and we screamed and laughed and videoed ourselves. I met Gyula here, a Hungarian filmmaker, his films banned in Hungary— a gentle, humble man who became a world-class director within the constraints of communism. There is a tenderness and generosity toward his subjects in his films, even if the subject is the ludicrousness of making art by committee or about a work camp for boys in high school where there is no work. My friend Geoff came to begin the translations of his grand-mother's letters from before their Jewish family was forced out of Berlin, their relatives killed in the camps. We visited a Jewish cemetery together where his great-uncle is buried. And then there were the children of Lynette's cousin, whom we had met only through social media. The entire family visited us—mom, dad, the little boy in princess costumes, who is seven now, and his five-year-old brother. The princess wore sparkles and we bought him a stuffed pony and a unicorn and he pirouetted through our apartment. The five-year-old and I played with superheroes donned in axes and shields, breathing fire and flames. I love being a man. I love learning from good men. I have enormous hope for boys who wear sparkles and maybe decide they are not boys, and boys who jump on trampolines, and boys in high school with no work, and men researching their past, and trans men who want to climb mountains. All of us connect in Berlin, all of us in various states of becoming, all of us with the right to become our best selves. I am them and they are me and we are all in this together.

I am looking out my window, the sun just rising over the lake, no sailboats yet. After the hottest summer on record in Boston and now Berlin, there is a bit of fall in the air, that soothing coolness that makes a body feel like there is one perfect temperature—fifty-eight degrees, I would argue, for this body. I can wear jeans and sneakers and a T-shirt with a long-sleeved shirt on top, unbuttoned and flung open, chest wide, and I can walk out into the city, feel my feet land solidly on the cobblestone sidewalks, rub my hand over my almost-full beard, and know that I am here.

SOURCES AND INSPIRATIONS

As a trans person, I spent most of my life with my head in a book imagining other lives, other bodies, and other histories. In some ways, my memoir is an amalgamation of all the books that kept me curious, kept me thinking it was worth it to keep going. Sometimes it was to dream myself a cowboy on the open prairie, sometimes a soldier with a rifle as tall as me, sometimes a priest giving other men hope of a God on the other side. But reading wasn't just about imagining myself a man; it was about imagining, period—imagining all parts of my identity until I could physically feel myself as a body alive in the world.

Here is sort of an acknowledgments section to literature and nonfiction and poetry—to the stories that bought me time and helped me to eventually see this body in the context of multiple histories and struggles, to eventually be seen and felt and heard. I owe these works of art, and the many others that I didn't have room to list, my life.

The Brothers Karamazov, Fyodor Dostoyevsky (1879, 1880). A novel that tells the story of three brothers and that engages all the major ethical debates—exploring faith, morality, free will, greed, obsession, and madness.

How many times have I read this book? How many times can you read a book this long? I am Ivan, in a constant state of doubt, always on the verge of a nervous breakdown, or not even on the verge. Reading *The Brothers Karamazov* is like being in the psych ward of your own mind—doubt, doubt, doubt, doubt, "I have a longing for life and I go on living in spite of logic." This is a trans person's motto. What logic is there living in a constant state of misrecognition? Who wouldn't, like Ivan, have a nervous breakdown? One time, close to another trip to the psych ward, I rented a cabin in northern Minnesota and read the novel in three days. Psych ward averted. Hikes, "sticky little leaves as they open in the spring," as Ivan would say, and Dostoyevsky. I went on living.

Great Expectations, Charles Dickens (1861). The coming-of-age story of an orphan named Pip raised by his not-so-kind sister, Mrs. Joe, and her gentle husband, the blacksmith Joe. Pip, thanks to an unknown benefactor, suddenly has prospects, and thus has a chance to become "uncommon."

Of course, as the daughter of a used-car salesman, I wanted nothing more than to become uncommon. Is a used-car salesman a comparable trade to a blacksmith? Was my mother my emotional Joe? I didn't dare fall in love like Pip. There was no Estella, but how often, like Pip, "did I dream that my expectations were all canceled"? I read *Great Expectations* over Christmas break of sixth grade. That Christmas we had tickets to fly to Orlando to go to Disney World. We had never had a family vacation, and four days prior my father was arrested for drunk driving, went to jail, and then to treatment for thirty days. We spent Christmas in Elkhart—Pip helped me to hang on to my hopes. At the end of the novel we see him walking hand in hand with Estella—maybe, just maybe, his love will finally be reciprocated. Maybe, just maybe, his greatest expectation will be realized.

Citizen: An American Lyric, Claudia Rankine (2014). Rankine has reinvented poetry in form and purpose and *Citizen* is a masterpiece that exposes in detail our America built at its roots in the violence and cruelty of white supremacy.

I once saw Claudia Rankine described as "the truth" on Twitter. When you read words strung together like this—"You take in things you don't want all the time. . . . Then the voice in your head silently tells you to take your foot off your throat because just getting along shouldn't be an ambition,"—"the truth" seems right. As I went through my gender transition, I had the privilege of working with Claudia on a play about whiteness, and it was impossible to lose track of what I was becoming—a white man. Not just a man, but a white man. I will never be able to stop accounting for what that symbolizes, for the history that my body carries. Claudia's poetry insists.

The Warmth of Other Suns, Isabel Wilkerson (2010). This book tells the story of the Great Migration of 1915 to 1970 of African Americans from the South to the Northeast, Midwest, and West through the lives of three people—a sharecropper's wife, a farmer, and a doctor.

I read this book when it came out in 2010. I was forty-four years old with a BA, an MA, and a PhD. How could I have known so little about this period of history? I felt embarrassed—a gap in my education as wide as the Grand Canyon. "Perhaps the greatest single act of family disruption and heartbreak among black Americans in the twentieth century was the result of the hard choices made by those on either side of the Great Migration." Wilkerson's account is staggering, with people's lives so fully realized that a history book of more than five hundred pages reads like a page-turner novel. This book single-handedly changed my understanding of race in contemporary America.

Blood Meridian, Cormac McCarthy (1985). It's hard to summarize this book. An ultra-violent western set in the mid-1800s with no moments of redemption, seen through the wanderings of "the kid."

Sometime in the early part of this century, I decided to read every book by Cormac McCarthy. I am always looking for a way to understand and eradicate my inner rage and violence, and reading McCarthy is like earning your PhD in white man's violence. In those unexpected moments when I resemble my father, unleash on the driver in front of me, say something horrible to my wife, become some version of every bad white man, I think of the kid saying to his friend Sproule, "What's wrong with you is wrong all the way through you." What's wrong with America is wrong all the way through. McCarthy shows us a nation that came into being through violence, a violence that lives in us all.

Sexing the Cherry, Jeanette Winterson (1989). This novel is about a mother named Dog Woman who has pockmarks on her face big enough to hold fleas, and her son, Jordan, who adores her. It is a fairy tale that subverts male power and questions the dichotomy of gender roles.

Jeanette Winterson's writing has been a life raft for queer people for more than thirty years. She was thinking about "nonbinary" as a gender possibility long before it became a recognized gender marker. *Sexing the Cherry* became the basis for one of the chapters of my doctoral dissertation as I compared women's studies and queer theory, as I considered if borders around gender constituted a more powerful way to make political change or if the fluidity of "queer" was more inclusive, more politically savvy. "Was I searching for a dancer whose name I did not know or was I searching for the dancing part of myself?" asks Dog Woman. *Sexing the Cherry* helped me to keep the dancing part of myself within reach.

A Farewell to Arms, Ernest Hemingway (1929). A love story between an American paramedic serving in the Italian Army, Frederic Henry, and an English nurse, Catherine Barkley. They meet near the Italian front where the Italians are eventually defeated and flee to Switzerland before Frederic is about to be executed in a purge of soldiers blamed for losing the battle.

In 1990, when I was doing my master's in peace studies at the University of Notre Dame, my colleagues were studying things like international law, conflict resolution, and nonviolent resistance. I created my own path reading war literature: *War and Peace, Mother Courage,* and *A Farewell to Arms*. It was perhaps *A Farewell to Arms* that turned me most resolutely against war and the men who orchestrated it. I loved Frederic, with his quiet devotion to both Catherine and the cause, and the mere thought that he would be held accountable for the Italians' poor military strategy demonstrated the emptiness of words like *conviction* and *loyalty* when it came to men and their weapons. The following summer I would get arrested for trespassing on government property while protesting at a naval nuclear weapons base in Southern California.

Their Eyes Were Watching God, Zora Neale Hurston (1937). This is the story of Janie Crawford, in her forties, retelling the story of her life to a friend, mostly an account of her relationships with various men who treat her like property, a "mule," until she meets her true love, Tea Cake.

I read this book in 1991, when I was working in Deland, Florida, with the children of Mexican union farmworkers. The novel takes place in Florida, partly in Eatonville, not too far from Deland. I read all of Hurston that year, determined to understand why her writing was dismissed by the authors of the Harlem Renaissance. Why had it taken almost forty years to recognize her genius, when she began to be read in Black Studies programs in the '70s and '80s? My work in Deland spiraled me into a deep depression—the poverty, the danger these young people faced, the lack of opportunity.

Hurston's rich language, her ability to capture the nothing-ness of Central Florida, and Janie's perseverance as African American men objectified her the way white men objectified them mirrored my sense of objectification by the Catholic Church, my employer at the time. I was not equating my plight as a white woman with Janie's, only acknowledging my gratitude to Hurston for writing so powerfully about the relentless reality of patriarchy and Janie's refusal to give up hope.

Gender Trouble, Judith Butler (1990). This is perhaps the most important book to upend all the preconceived tenets of feminism that had come prior, arguing against identity politics contending both sex and gender are cultural constructs, performances etched in the body.

I started my PhD in the fall of 1991 in cultural studies and this book was my bible. I bought a pair of men's black jeans, a blue denim men's shirt, and a blue flower tie and delivered my first academic lecture on the movie *Thelma & Louise* and its subversion of what constituted women's behavior, Butler leading the way. *Gender Trouble* denies the "before" within feminist theory and therefore any notion of an "authentic feminine." Gun-toting Thelma and Louise were my anti-feminine heroes while I began to rethink the possibilities for my own body.

Lyndon Johnson and the American Dream, Doris Kearns Goodwin (1991). This is a heartfelt biography of Lyndon Johnson.

I read this book for the first time two years ago. I owe it the biggest insight I've had to date on what is at the heart of white masculinity—conviction. In fact, Johnson refused to end the Vietnam War because of his own conviction and despite the advice of almost all the experts surrounding him. We all know where that conviction got us.

Go, Went, Gone, Jenny Erpenbeck (translated by Susan Bernofsky, 2017). This book tells the story of Richard, a retired German professor of the classics who slowly becomes deeply involved in the lives of a group of African refugees in Berlin.

Richard wonders, "How many times . . . must a person relearn everything he knows, rediscovering it over and over . . . Is a human lifetime long enough?" I have spent my lifetime trying to understand "otherness." I am on the top of everyone's list when they need someone to sit on a panel or committee about "diversity." I am a go-to "other." This book, layer by layer, exposed to me the impossibility of inhabiting a body that is not mine, feeling a culture that is not mine, helping in circumstances that exist miles away from my own experience. As ridiculous as talk of border walls is, committing to connect across difference is a lifetime's work. Borders live in all of us.

My Name is Lucy Barton, Elizabeth Strout (2016). A novel about a mother and daughter reconnecting to each other.

As Lucy is recovering from an infection in the hospital, she says, "It was the sound of my mother's voice I most wanted; what she said didn't matter." It was this very sound I thought might save me at numerous points in my life. This is a book about everything left unsaid, the book that forced me to say I would have to relinquish the hope of reconnecting to my mother.

A Field Guide to Getting Lost, Rebecca Solnit (2005). A meditation on all the ways to get lost and all the emotions that come in those moments when we aren't quite certain where we are.

"To what degree has anxiety replaced optimism?" Solnit asks as she considers the early explorers and the optimistic way they approached the unknown, the possibility of what they might find. This book is my most popular teaching tool, as the majority of my students are crippled by anxiety, obsessed with finding their way in a direct shot from point A to point B. I get it. I have been no less influenced by a culture that insists we know where we are headed. This book was my meditation tool during my gender transition. I had no idea where I was going or where I would end up. "Never to get lost is not to live . . ." I have done a lot living in the last few years.

The New Jim Crow, Michelle Alexander (2010). An account of the mass incarceration of African American men and the subsequent creation of a new caste system that uses the legal system to keep black men as second-class citizens who, as a result of either being locked up or having criminal records, are denied basic civil rights, including the right to vote, the right to serve on juries, and the right to attain affordable housing.

I read this book when it came out in 2010. I was working in a theater in Chicago as the director of artistic development and planning what would be the following season. We planned a season based on the theme of race. All five plays selected were about race—and all five were written by white men. I couldn't take in what *The New Jim Crow* was exposing and defend that season. Thanks to that book, I quit my job at the theater.

Three Steps on the Ladder of Writing, Hélène Cixous (1993). This is a book about writing that explores three necessary "schools" for great writing to be possible: the School of the Dead, the School of Dreams, and the School of Roots.

I have been reading and teaching this book for years. It scares me. "*It is the feeling of secret* we become acquainted with when we dream, that is what makes us enjoy and at the same time fear dreaming." To write is to dream. To write is to risk everything, to bring what is buried to the surface. I had to read this book perhaps five times as I wrote my memoir, to say out loud what I had kept hidden from myself, to tell you secrets that I swore I would not remember.

Road Trip, Lynette D'Amico (2015). This is a novella about two friends who travel across Minnesota and Wisconsin together, veering off track more than once.

This is my wife's novella. I have been reading her writing for twenty-two years. When we were first introduced, I was told she was a writer and I knew immediately I could not date someone who was just "okay" at telling stories, so I tracked down one of her essays, "Home Movies." It was hilarious and beautifully written and we started dating. Lynette has been my partner in all things creative for twenty-two years, and *Road Trip* is a perfect example of Lynette's imagination and talent. I wouldn't be a writer if it weren't for her, for us.

The Lord of the Rings, J. R. R. Tolkien (1954, first published as a trilogy). A fantasy trilogy that includes *The Fellowship of the Ring*, *The Two Towers*, and *The Return of the King*. It is about the search for a ring that has the power to rule the world.

The summer after seventh grade was, in Dickensian terms, the best of times and the worst of times. I had been kicked out of Catholic school and was going to start eighth grade in the public school. I had put on weight, a fleshy blob whose clothes suddenly didn't fit. I had no friends. But *The Lord of the Rings* saved me from complete misery. I laid on our worn green couch next to the big tear in our worn green carpet in the living room and I read all three books of the trilogy—1,241 pages plus *The Hobbit*, another 304 pages. I almost never looked up. I walked the entire distance of Middle Earth in my imagination. Elkhart, Indiana? Where was that?

Jesus' Son, Denis Johnson (1992). A linked short story collection about the travels of a drug-addicted hitchhiker named Fuckhead.

I have never had an issue with drugs. I don't relate to Fuckhead's addictions. I just loved the utter chaos of this book, its structure and language. "With each step my heart broke for the person I would never find, the person who would love me." Growing up in a house of abuse and neglect, I never felt I could be loved. I couldn't feel love. I still struggle to feel love. This is what Fuckhead and I had in common. The hole in the soul of the addict is much like the hole in the soul of someone abused.

Angels in America, Tony Kushner (1991). A two-part play about AIDS and homosexuality and politics and power.

This remarkable and epic piece of storytelling has many pieces that drew me to it, but I hold on to it almost thirty years after its premiere because it is such a profound lesson about bodies—their secretions and wounds and sexual preferences. Louis is a character who is all head and politics and when his lover's body begins to ooze and decay, he walks away. His terror of the flesh is my terror.

Bluets, Maggie Nelson (2009). A prose poem about all things blue.

"Nonetheless, as Billie Holiday knew, it remains the case that to see blue in deeper and deeper saturation is eventually to move toward darkness." I love this little cultish book, the blue of despair, loss, depression, and loneliness sitting side by side with the beautiful blue of the sea and sky. The roaming of a life in relationship to a color, my favorite color. Nelson's writing lets me be sad and soothed, hopeful and despairing.

Open City, Teju Cole (2011). A character, Julius, wanders through New York.

I have always liked the word *peregrinations*, and the prose of this stream-of-consciousness novel defines it. This is a book about walking, walking without purpose or regulations. Its language is a kind of improvisation. I read it when I was walking every morning with my wife in a cemetery in Boston, trying to get up the courage to walk away from something I thought I might do forever. "To be alive it seemed to me, as I stood there in all kinds of sorrow, was to be both original and reflection, and to be dead was to be split off, to be reflection alone." Toxic masculinity had poisoned my workplace. I felt dead for sixty hours a week, relegated to someone else's reflection, but peregrinations through cemeteries, arboretums, and white mountains brought me back to my original half.

The Sixth Extinction, Elizabeth Kolbert (2014). A book that argues we are in the sixth extinction, in a state of dire environmental decline marked by the disappearance of native species at an unprecedented rate.

This book presents us with the biggest danger facing our planet. Kolbert tells it in a way that's easy to follow. It's a book that should make us drop everything we are doing and commit ourselves to our survival as a species through environmental activism. What gender I am won't matter when humans no longer exist. I once heard Kolbert lecture. She began by saying, "When I am finished, the first thing you will want to ask me is 'What should I do?' I am going to tell you now, I don't know." When she finished her lecture, a man immediately raised his hand and said, "So, what should we do?" This book is like a persistent echo in the back of my mind: What should I do? What should I do? What should I do?

ACKNOWLEDGMENTS

Thank you to Claudia Rankine, who insisted I write down what was happening to me as I transitioned a life. Thank you to Lee Pelton, Sylvia Spears, Michaele Whelan, and Rob Sabal of Emerson College, an institution with the best people, who understand what it means to be an artist and to support a colleague through a nearly impossible life change at age fifty-two. Many thanks to my amazing students at Emerson; they make me yearn for what's ahead and challenge me to do better for the sake of their futures.

Every trans person needs at least two attorneys to be acknowledged as a full human being; mine—Rachel Stroup and Caitlin Egleson—were the very best. On top of lawyers, you need an entire professional care team who refuses to let you believe your life is any less valuable than the cis person sitting next to you. Thank you, LeAnn. I love you so much. And to Chase, I have learned the definition of a good man from you. Fenway Health Center and Dr. Lauren Scott make Boston the best place to be a trans person. Dr. Cristina Cusin, you gave me new life. And to my trainer, Alex—that day you told me to rub my body hard with a towel before getting in the pool so I could feel the support of the water against my skin gave me a new image for how I wanted to live moving forward.

Time, space, and financial support is imperative to the creative process. Thank you to the Ford Foundation Art of Change Fellowship, the American Academy in Berlin, the University of Washington in Seattle, Todd London and the Andrew W. Mellon Creative Research Residency, the Mass Cultural Council, and Nancy Allen in Taos.

Every guy needs a couple of buddies to hike with and drink beer with and talk sneakers with. Thank you, Lee Schere, for your most enduring friendship, and my newest best buddy, Corey Shields. You both make life infinitely more fun.

And then to all the incredible women in my life, especially Mary McGreevy, Susan Feder, Holly Sidford, Hannalore Tice, and then to all the artistic collaborators who have dreamed the theater with me: Diane Paulus, Lisa D'Amour, Joanna Settle, Sarah Ruhl, Melanie Marnich, Deborah Stein, Suli Holum, Anne García Romero, Lisa Portes, and a hundred more people who belong here.

Thank you to my brothers, Tim and Christian, for surviving our family with me, for the work you both do to be your best selves in your own families, and for maintaining a connection between us. You are my family and I love you both.

Thank you to Ira Silverberg for believing in this book at the proposal stage and editing it with so much care and love, and to Jonathan Cox and Jonathan Karp and everyone at Simon & Schuster who has embraced my story. You aren't just publishing a memoir, but affirming the reality of trans lives as a vital part of the American landscape.

I'm not a religious guy, but sometimes an angel falls from the sky and elevates your sense of what you are capable of. Frances Coady is an agent who has made me a better writer. I don't know how she has time to represent other writers, because she has labored over every word of this book multiple times and has been there through every step of this process. She defines the word pro.

Lynette, I know there were many days we both wondered if we would still be together when the book was published, but damn if we aren't still here. You didn't sign up for this. You knew from the moment a person knows that you wanted to spend your life with a woman. I am so honored that despite that, you loved me enough to make room in your life for a man, that you stayed. I love your hair, your smile, your cooking, your generosity, your beautiful writing, and being your husband is my greatest life accomplishment. The memoir was only possible because you were by my side, reading every word, fighting through the pain and grief and loss with me, and proving that our love is even deeper than gender. I am with you always.

P. CARL is a Senior Distinguished Artist-in-Residence at Emerson College in Boston, Massachusetts, and was awarded a 2017 Art of Change fellowship from the Ford Foundation; the Berlin Prize fellowship from the American Academy in Berlin for fall 2018; the Andrew W. Mellon Creative Research Residency at the University of Washington; and the Anschutz Distinguished Fellowship at Princeton University for spring 2020. He made theater for twenty years and now writes, teaches, travels, mountain climbs, and swims. He resides in the Jamaica Plain neighborhood of Boston with his wife, the writer Lynette D'Amico; and their dogs, Lenny and Sonny.